Selling Radio Direct

RELATED FOCAL PRESS TITLES

Selling Radio Direct

Michael C. Keith

Foreword by Wayne Cornils

Focal Press
Boston   London

Focal Press is an imprint of Butterworth-Heinemann.

Recognizing the importance of preserving what has been written, it
is the policy of Butterworth-Heinemann to have the books it
publishes printed on acid-free paper, and we exert our best efforts to
that end.

Library of Congress Cataloging-in-Publication Data
Keith, Michael C.
   Selling radio direct / by Michael C. Keith.
     p. cm.
   Includes bibliographical references.
   ISBN 0-240-80091-5 (alk. paper)
   1. Radio advertising.   I. Title.   II. Series.
HF6146.R3K453   1992   91-37959
659.14′2′0688—dc20   CIP

British Library Cataloguing in Publication Data

Keith, Michael C
   Selling radio direct

   I. Title   II. Series
   791.440232

   ISBN 0-240-80091-5

Butterworth-Heinemann
80 Montvale Avenue
Stoneham, MA 02180

10 9 8 7 6 5 4 3 2

Printed in the United States of America

This book is dedicated to all radio sales reps far and wide, to those generous people quoted within these covers, and to those experts greater than I—Wayne Cornils, Jay Williams, Eric Rhoads, Dave Gifford, Alan Cimberg, and Ken Costa.

Contents

Foreword

Sooner or later all selling comes down to eyeball-to-eyeball, mind-to-mind, person-to-person communication. In advertising, and especially radio, there is a fringe which would reduce the profession to a pseudo-science of computer generated numbers.

Computer driven robots build cars, but people sell cars. Computer software programs design and build computers, but men and women still sell computers.

Radio stations, like people, have individual personalities, and personalities don't compute very well. The subtle differences between stations, markets, on-air talent, and promotion and marketing support capabilities are difficult—if not impossible—to accurately portray in computer language.

So, if I (the buyer) decide that I don't like your format, you (the seller) tell me "That's okay because your radio station is not programmed for me. Your radio station is programmed for the hundreds, or thousands, or tens-of-thousands of listener-consumers who daily give us their ears and minds and access to their spendable income."

The performance of the profession of radio sales can be likened to the scales of justice. The salesperson's goal is to pile up a sufficient number of benefits on the right side of the scale to offset the negatives (cost) that the buyer has placed on the left side of the scale. When the benefits outweigh the negatives, the sale is made. The buyer gets the benefits and the salesperson gets the commission.

In this book, Michael Keith relates the intricacies of how and why the system works. Selling radio direct (person-to-person) is and will continue to be the heart of radio sales in small and medium markets and is rapidly becoming the standard even in large markets. Selling radio advertising is selling concepts, ideas, excitement, and minds. Selling radio is people selling people and machines cannot do that—only people interacting on each other's hearts and minds can do that.

Wayne Cornils

(Mr. Cornils is former senior vice president of radio for the National Association of Broadcasters and former executive vice president of the Radio Advertising Bureau.)

1

Time Is Money

"Remember, that time is money"
Advice to a Young Tradesman—Ben Franklin

Many people have considered time selling a strange occupation. Time is an abstract concept, and here you are expected to sell it to the owner of the local hardware store:

"Hi, I'm Bill from X109, and I'm here to sell you *time*."

"Great, young fella'!" replies the elderly store proprietor, truly pleased that you have taken *time* from your hectic schedule to offer him the chance of a life*time*. "I'd like about 20 years to tack onto the 68 I've already spent on this planet."

No problem," responds the *time* seller, knowing a sale when he sees one. "Just sign here. That'll be 10 dollars a minute, sir."

"Whoa! Wait just a second, sonny. You mean to tell me if I buy 20 years from your station, it'll cost me 10 dollars every minute?"

"But, sir," counters the young *time* vendor, detecting resistance from his would-be client, "we're the number one station in town!"

"Let's see," calculates the merchant, "that figures to $14,400 a day…"

"And well worth it, sir, because no other station gives you the numbers we do."

"I'll say!" exclaims the old man intently calculating.

"In the latest ratings survey, X109 is tops in over 50-year-old females…"

"$100,800 a week…"

"And number one in all dayparts Sundays. We've got the best ski reports, sports reports, weather reports, consumer reports, traffic reports, stock reports…"

"$403,208 a month…"

"Farm reports, world reports, local reports, and we can guarantee you fixed *times* in Triple A, Double A, Single A, and bonus availabilities (don't tell my boss) on a BTA basis in B *time* or ROS you three bonus availabilities in overnights…"

"$4,838,400 a year…"

"Not to mention the fact that because you're buying a long term contract, which results in an annual bulk rate, you'll get a discount which, if you're smart, you'll apply to the purchase of X109's weekend satellite concert special…"

"$96,768,000 for 20 years!"

"Is that a great deal or what? If you'll give me your John Hancock, we'll set the clock in motion, sir."

"Forget it, son. *Time* on your station just costs too darn much."

At least Willy Loman had a tangible to sell. Everyone understands shoes. But you're a *time* salesperson, and your stock in trade is called the *spot*. Now that's almost as curious an item as *time* itself. A double whammy. You're a *time* salesperson looking for a *spot* buyer. You sell *spots* of *time*—little evocative soundbites traversing the vast expanses of space at the speed of light. A strange occupation but unique as well. In fact, there's no other occupation quite like radio sales, and for those individuals who possess the so-called *right stuff*, no other quite as rewarding.

The goal of the following pages is to offer the practicing (or soon to be) radio sales rep (representative) information needed to succeed in this challenging profession. But first, a little history review.

SELLING TIME FROM THE START

To many early radio proponents, the idea of selling airtime seemed unfitting, if not downright blasphemous. In the 1920s, Department of Commerce Secretary Herbert Hoover served as the quasi-official overseer of the fledgling medium, and he perceived the use of the airwaves for commercial enterprise as a rather corrupt notion. He contended that it would be a shame if an instrument with such potential for public good were to become a venue for profiteers, and many agreed with him, including one senator who foresaw radio as a *pawnshop of the air*. Thus, broadcasters were reluctant to go full-throttle in the direction of commercialism.

One of the world's largest corporations, AT&T, happened to be in the broadcast business, and they did not ignore the lure of the dollar. Its flagship station, WEAF in New York, was the first to air a commercial announcement in 1921. The station charged a Queens real estate corporation $50 for what it called ten minutes of *tollcasting*. The AT&T-owned station viewed the use of airtime by commercial ventures as analogous to its parent company charging its telephone customers a toll for long distance calls.

The effort proved a success, and within a few months the station had attracted other tollcasting customers. Despite AT&T's attempt to copyright the tollcasting concept, many stations, in dire need of a source of income (unlike WEAF), began leasing airtime. Yet, the watchful scrutiny of Mr. Hoover and his supporters kept overt on-air advertising to a minimum. In fact, stations used a technique known as *indirect* advertising (program sponsorship/underwriting). This permitted stations to generate income by providing clients a name mention before and after a particular program, that is, a specific tie-in with a program. For example, "Good Evening ladies and gentlemen, and welcome to the 'Eveready Battery Hour,' and at the show's conclusion, "That's it for tonight folks. We hope you've enjoyed the 'Eveready Battery Hour.' Tune in again next week." No commercials were inserted in the program.

By the late 1920s and early 1930s, however, broadcasters threw caution to the wind and signed clients as fast as they could for *direct* advertising. Soon the bleak prophesy of the senator who opposed radio commercialism was fulfilled as the medium began to sound like a *pawnshop*. Without adequate regulation governing the nature and credibility of products and services promoted by advertisers, the airwaves were rampant with false claims and bogus promises. Eventually, the Federal Trade Commission and the newly formed Federal Communications Commission saw fit to assert itself on the matter and laws were established to prevent on-air hucksterism. However, direct advertising (commercial announcements of one to several minutes in duration) became an accepted, or at least tolerated, fact of life.

The United States, unlike a myriad of other countries, chose the path of entrepreneurial broadcasting. Had this not been the case, and the United States had chosen to remain a noncommercial venture, the field of broadcast sales would not exist (nor would this book). We are the most prominent broadcasting enterprise on earth, and it would be hard to imagine it being so without it having become a part of that lusty and dynamic machine called *capitalism.*

Every ideology has its false starts, and capitalism has had its share, but certainly none as catastrophic as the stock market crash and ensuing Depression in the 1930s. However, radio did more than just survive. Network salespeople and ad agencies were kept busy. The public's desire for radio fare grew in almost direct proportion to the economy's slump. People wanted to escape the unpleasant realities of the failed economy, and radio could make this possible, without cost.

Since the majority of the population had a radio set in the 1930s, all it had to do was flick the switch and worlds of wonderful distraction flowed forth. Businesses interested in effectively reaching the public (it is a misnomer that all businesses went belly-up after the crash) recognized a good thing. People flocked to their radios, rather than the movie or vaudeville houses—they cost money. Advertisers were virtually offered a captive audience by the broadcast medium.

Concern that ad agencies played too great a role in network programming decisions reached a boiling point. For many years, the major advertising agencies had literally dictated programming. The agencies not only had the clients but they also designed their programs before going to the networks. Essentially, the networks aired what the agencies brought to them. They could either accept the programs or reject them. Of course, the latter decision meant no income. Following the government's intervention, ad agencies were put out of the programming business. Unofficially, however, ad agencies continued to exert enormous influence in the areas of network programming and scheduling.

As the Depression's grip loosened in the late 1930s, many more stations entered the airwaves. Concomitantly, radio sales became an even more viable career option. There was money to be made peddling airtime, and many sales people found that success in sales significantly increased their chances for management jobs and even station ownership.

The fortunes of radio continued during World War II. In fact, the medium's status and credibility grew, which only heightened its desirability as an advertising tool. Though this time it was not to escape the terrible realities of world affairs, but rather to tune them in.

Listeners wanted every bit of information they could gather about the war, and the networks responded by dramatically increasing their coverage of the global conflict. Thus, audiences grew as did advertiser use of the medium. Programs sold out. Radio became the first source of news and information about the war for most Americans, and that translated to economic prosperity.

Meanwhile, the production values in commercials became more sophisticated as the medium matured. The straight, no-frills announcements of the 1920s gave way to a variety of styles and approaches in the 1930s, among these the dramatization, testimonial, and singing commercial (jingle). All or most of these were presented live, and audiences seldom tuned them out. As much attention was paid to commercials as to the programs in which they were slotted, and this made advertisers quite happy. The radio salesperson had magic and entertainment to sell.

"Hello, ma'am, I'm from WXXX. The station that brings you all those great shows each night."

"Really? Say, that's right. We listen to our favorite show on your station."

"So how'd you like to be on our broadcasts? Let everybody know what a great little hat shop you have here?"

"You mean that my store can be heard on the 'Neal Kenton Ballroom Hour?' Oh, I bet that would be very expensive, wouldn't it?"

"Not at all, ma'am. In fact, all your friends and customers can hear about your store for no more than it costs to run an average size ad in the local newspaper."

"Why, gee wiz, isn't that just the cat's pizazz. How do I get on?"

Keep in mind we're talking 1930. Times have changed, and radio isn't perceived as that wonderful magic medium by most retailers as it once was. Of course, many who use radio effectively today would argue that it still possesses considerable magic.

Radio and its salespeople continued to prosper throughout the 1940s, but the medium began to encounter some disturbing turbulence as the nation became infatuated with television later in the decade. By the early 1950s, television had usurped radio's place as the foremost home entertainment medium. Radio went into a mild tailspin before it reinvented itself, stressing targeted programming and mobility. By the mid-1950s, most radio salespeople were selling commercials in deejay music shows on stations that programmed to preselected audiences. That has been pretty much the case every since.

By design, this has been a very brief overview of selling time from the start. For a more detailed account of the evolution of broadcasting consult *The Broadcast Century: A Biography of American Broadcasting* by me and Robert Hilliard (Focal Press, 1992).

STATION ORGANIZATION: WHERE YOU FIT IN

A radio station is composed of several areas (see Figure 1), all of which fall into at least one of three categories: sales, programming, and engineering. These areas interact with one another, particularly sales. A salesperson is in daily contact with many station personnel: the production person and traffic director to name two. In addition, each department has a supervisor. What follows gives you an idea of the responsibilities of these individuals:

Program Director (PD): One of the three key department head positions at most radio stations, the PD is responsible for developing and executing the format, hiring and managing air staff, establishing the schedule of airshifts, monitoring the station to ensure consistency and quality of product, keeping abreast of competition and

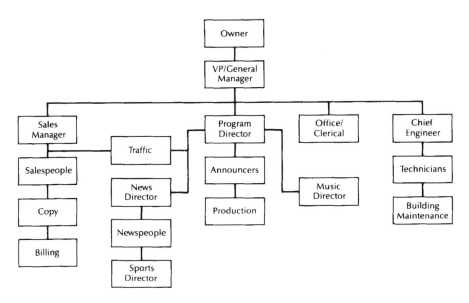

▶ *Figure 1*   *Organizational flow chart for a medium market radio station.*

trends that may affect programming, maintaining the music library, complying with FCC rules and regulations, and directing the efforts of the news and public affairs areas.

Chief Engineer (CE): The CEs responsibilities include operating the station within prescribed technical parameters established by the FCC, purchasing/repairing/maintaining equipment, monitoring signal fidelity, adapting studios for programming needs, setting up remote broadcast operations, and working closely with the programming department.

Since the topic of this book is radio sales, we'll devote more time to a description of the role of the station's sales department head. The sales manager or general sales manager directs the marketing of the radio station's airtime. This person is responsible for moving inventory, which in the radio outlet constitutes the selling of spot and feature schedules to advertisers. The sales manager directs the daily efforts of the station's sales staff (called account executives [AEs]), establishes sales department policies, develops sales plans and materials, conceives of sales and marketing campaigns and promotions, sets quotas, and also may sell. Some sales managers prefer to keep selling even when it isn't required in order to stay in touch, while others prefer to invest their time in other ways.

The organizational structure of a station's sales department customarily includes the positions of national, regional, and local sales managers. The national responsibilities usually are handled by the general sales manager. This includes working with the station's rep company to stimulate business from national advertisers. The regional sales manager (not every station has this designation, although someone on the sales staff will oversee regional accounts) explores sales possibilities in a broad geographical area surrounding the station. For example, the regional person for an outlet in New York City may be assigned portions of Connecticut, New Jersey, and Long Island while the station's local sales manager would concentrate on advertisers within the city proper. The General sales manager oversees the efforts of each individual and at small stations may personally be involved with account acquisitions on the national, regional, and local levels.

The size of a station's sales staff varies according to its location and reach. A typical small market radio station employs between two and four account executives, while the medium market station (those in areas with populations between 100 and 500 thousand) averages about five. Large, top-ranked metropolitan outlets may employ as many as eight to ten salespeople, although it is more typical for a big market station to have about a half-dozen people account hunting.

The general sales manager reports directly to the station's general manager and works closely with the program director in developing salable features. Regular daily and weekly sales meetings are scheduled and conducted by the sales manager, during which time goals are set and problems addressed. The sales manager also assigns account lists to members of the staff and helps coordinate trade and co-op sales (discussed in Chapter 13).

The head of the sales department is usually responsible for maintaining close contact with the station's rep company as a way of generating income from national advertisers, who are handled by advertising agencies. The relationship of the sales manager and rep company is a particularly important one, since a large part of a station's business may result from this cooperative venture. Small stations often have less involvement with rep companies, since fewer national advertisers earmark dollars for this area. In addition, the sales manager must be adept at working ratings figures to the station's advantage for inclusion in sales promotional materials that are used on both the national and local sales levels.

All sales come under the scrutiny of the sales manager, who determines if an account is appropriate for the station and whether conditions of the sale meet established standards. In addition, the sales manager may have a policy that requires credit checks to be made on every new account and that each new client pay for a portion of his schedule up front as a show of good faith. Policies vary from station to station.

It is up to the head of sales to keep abreast of local and national sales and marketing trends that can be used to the station's advantage. This requires that the sales manager constantly survey trade magazines, like *The Pulse of Radio* and *Advertising Age*, and general publications, such as *USA Today*, *Business Week*, *Money*, and *The Wall Street Journal*, and attend industry seminars, such as those conducted by the Radio Advertising Bureau (RAB) and the National Association of Broadcasters (NAB). No sales department can operate in a vacuum and hope to succeed in todays' dynamic radio marketplace.

Now you have an idea of what your boss does. It is incumbent on the salesperson to learn who does what at the station. There should be no grey areas. This is rule number one in the *know your product* category. To give you an idea of how the sales rep interacts with station personnel here is a common scenario:

Mary has just landed a client. The signature is on the contract and a song is in her heart. She returns to the station the conquering hero. Few sensations rival a successful sales presentation—the heralded close. At the station, the receptionist informs Mary that another client has called and wants her to return the call ASAP. Uh oh, Mary thinks, trouble in paradise? This particular client has a history for being somewhat unpredictable. Just last month after buying a heavy schedule, this same client decided he wanted all his spots shifted to midday, and then a day later wanted nothing but evenings and weekends. Mary was forced to get tough and read the client the riot act. No more revisions without proper notice, etc. This had silenced the client up 'til now. Now what? Once she has processed her new order she will return the client's call. Maybe it's not so bad, she thinks. Reminding herself that one of the jobs of the sales rep is to service the account, something she does very conscientiously. Now Mary informs her sales manager about her conquest.

"Signed Romar's Deli for two fixed 60's in 'Billy's Wake up Show.'"

"Good going! What's the frequency, and how many weeks?" asks the smiling sales manager.

"Monday through Thursday, for 6 weeks," answers Mary.

"Not bad. Couldn't get them for 12, eh?"

"Got all they had to give," responds Mary, thinking her boss an ungrateful cur, but realizing it is his job to both praise and push people on to greatness.

The sales manager inspects the contract and returns it approved to Mary, who now heads to the station's traffic person (the logger of spots and typist of contracts) to begin the processing of her order. With this accomplished, she writes the spot for Romar's based on the fact sheet she assembled on site. Forty-five minutes later she takes the written spot, accompanied by a production order form, to the station's program director, who assigns production jobs to members of the on-air staff.

"Why don't you give this to Johnny. He's in the production room right now," suggests the PD.

"Okay," responds Mary, who then heads to production.

Mary finds Johnny in the middle of a complex edit when she enters and consequently receives a barely perceptible nod as a greeting. A few minutes later Johnny has accomplished his edit.

"Kyle sent me in here to ask you to voice and mix this. When you're done, please call the client and play it for final approval."
Johnny grunts an acknowledgment, and Mary departs. Despite his lack of interpersonal skills, she admires and trusts Johnny's abilities in the production room. She knows the job will be done well. Before leaving the station to make a sales call, Mary visits the engineer to get batteries for her cassette machine, which she uses to play spec spots for clients.

"Need a couple of batteries, Howie."

"Mary, how goes it? Boy, I think you eat batteries."

"I do. That's why I've got *acid* indigestion."

Mary and the engineer exchange a few more pleasantries and then she is on her way to her appointment.

In the hour and 15 minutes Mary has spent at the station, she has dealt with several people, all of whom play a vital role in her ability to succeed. Moral: treat others as you would have them treat you.

UPWARD MOBILITY

Success in the field often leads to an office with your very own door. If you want to move up the corporate ladder or station organizational flow chart, sales is the place to start.

Statistics continue to show that sales people are most often recruited to fill management positions—station manager. Of course, you must first perform heroically on the field of battle. Those who reach the exec (executive) level are proven performers, or warriors. They have withstood the test by defying the odds. They have built a clientele that generates impressive commissions. They have shown themselves to be self-starters, with positive attitudes and strong interpersonal skills, among a host of other qualities that are discussed in more detail in the last chapter.

The bottom line is *you gotta want it real bad.* If you are easily satisfied, you won't make it in sales. Forget taking over the boss's office. The advice from those who occupy those posh, upper-level offices is simple: "stay hungry!" The salesperson who rewards herself with the rest of the day off after making a sale, just ends up with the rest of the day off.

The job market for radio salespeople has always been good. Every station is interested in someone who produces or who shows promise. There are nearly 10 thousand commercial stations out there, and it is probably safe to say most would make room for someone who exhibits the right stuff. What constitutes the legendary right stuff is the subject of this book. So hang in there.

If you're reading this chapter, chances are you're fairly new to the field. You have a lot of questions that this text answers. First, most entry-level sales jobs exist at smaller stations, and that may well be where you are right now. That's great! There's no place like the smaller station for learning the profession of radio sales. Why? Because you're learning from the ground up. You do it all, and that is the best way to become familiar with your product—radio.

Small stations can be wonderful places to work (I can personally attest to this, having spent a number of fulfilling years as a sales rep at rural outlets). The small station is typically located in towns and cities of under 100 thousand population, so you get to know everybody in the business community after a while, and that engenders business. A salesperson should be an actively involved citizen and member in good standing in the community. This can be rewarding in a number of ways. In sales, contacts are vital. Who you meet after hours can be just as important as who you meet during business hours. Forget the notion of *normal* business hours. A good radio salesperson stays *tuned in* around the clock.

Of course, there is nothing wrong with setting your sites on a larger station, where the earning potential may be greater. But the *big* station usually looks for a track record. Doing well at the small station will certainly help open doors to the bigger market station, which often offers its own unique rewards. This is not to suggest that big dollars can only be made in Metropolis. There are many small station AEs making a handsome annual income, and keep in mind too that the cost of living in Smalltown is generally lower. The bottom line is consider all the pros and cons before making the leap.

2

Selling Direct and Otherwise

The medium draws its sales from three levels—national, local, and direct (retail). Obviously, the focus of this book is direct sales. However, to understand the radio station sales department, an AE must be familiar with every level of sales. This chapter will first describe local and national sales and then present a discussion of direct sales.

LOCAL SALES

Stations derive income from area advertising agencies. The local agencies handle accounts that primarily exist in and around the reach of the station's signal. That is to say, local agencies place ad dollars on media for local and regional businesses. Generally speaking, the larger businesses in an area are most apt to sign on with a local agency, because they may have a larger advertising budget and wish to promote their wares in several media. For example, a local or regional retail outlet with eight locations might well be interested in newspaper, television, and radio advertising to reach the largest potential population in and around its stores. This is not to say that local agencies avoid signing small mom 'n' pop shops. But, as a general rule, agencies are set up to deal with budgets larger than a tiny enterprise allocates for promotion. From a radio station's prospective this is fine, because it uncomplicates things on the direct/retail sales level.

Local agencies do place dollars on radio, but sometimes rather sparingly. It is a statistical reality that local ad agencies go more to print than to air. However, a radio station can derive good revenue from buys made by local agencies. Radio generates around 10 billion dollars annually, and two-thirds of this comes from other-than-national-level buys. Of course, the bulk of that figure stems from action on the direct/retail front, but local buys are very important.

Local agencies reflect national agencies in how they handle accounts. For instance, agency reps (the equivalent of radio sales reps) hit the streets in an effort to sign clients, who are interested in promoting their enterprises to the public. Local agencies devise marketing plans for clients and tailor messages to bring those plans to fruition. The agency's media buyer decides where to allocate the client's funds—that is, how much to spend on what media. As indicated earlier, this may mean a radio buy, or the media buyer may determine that another medium is more suitable. This decision is commonly based on a variety of information at the buyer's disposal.

The station account exec assigned an agency to pitch will deal with the media buyer in a effort to convince them that X109 is a *must* buy. New sales people are seldom given agencies to pitch, because this usually involves a more sophisticated type of presentation—often with ratings numbers and marketing data.

The rate of commission derived from agency selling is less than from the direct side. Commission on direct/retail sales is typically somewhere between 12% and 15%, whereas commission from agency sales is in the vicinity of 10%.

The sales manager designates who receives what agency from which to solicit business. The criteria used generally is indicative of the time a person has spent on the job and how well that person is doing. In other words, agencies are *awarded* to those who appear to be heading in the right direction (to those who produce, or who appear capable of producing, on the direct level). Agencies are not assigned to sales-people who do not exhibit the potential to make the most from the assignment. At many small stations, agency business is regarded as the gravy on the meat and pota-toes that are represented by direct sales.

NATIONAL SALES

National sales are derived from agencies that handle the advertising needs of wide-reaching enterprises, such as McDonalds and General Motors. These agencies are found mostly in the country's major metropolitan centers, like New York, Los Angeles, Chicago, Detroit, and so on. Again, national agencies function much the same way as local agencies. They have account reps who seek new clients, mar-keting and creative people who work on promotional campaigns, and media buyers who place client dollars. The obvious difference is size. National agencies, like BBDO, employ hundreds, whereas the staff size of the local agency is often similar to that of the area radio station.

The Station's sales manager generally oversees national sales and seldom pitches these agencies directly. That is the job of the station's rep company, and it is the responsibility of the sales manager to work closely with this satellite sales force. In most cases, the sales manager does not receive commission, per se, from national sales cultivated by rep companies. However, the sales manager may have an agree-ment with the station whereby the sales manager receives a percentage of gross sta-tion sales. Each station strikes its own deal with its department heads.

National business is certainly important to a radio station. Typically, the larger the station the more national business it attracts. For example, top-rated metro market outlets may rely heavily on national sales to the extent that half their income comes from that level of sales. This rarely is the case at the small market station, where a much lower percentage of sales revenues (10% to 15%) stems from its national sales effort.

However, national business is important to small stations, since buys are often robust—substantial in rate and frequency. National buys often call for a heavy spot schedule in a station's prime daypart and at top of the card rates. Stations usually have a separate rate card for national business whereby the fee for airtime is adjusted up.

REP COMPANIES

Rep companies are the industry's middlemen(women). They are given the task of convincing national agency buyers to place dollars on the radio stations they represent. Without their existence, radio stations would have to find a way to reach the myriad of agencies on their own—an impossible task.

With few exceptions, radio outlets contract the services of a station rep company. Again, even the most diminutive station wants to be included in buys on the national level. The rep company basically is an extension of a station's sales department. The rep and the station's sales manager work closely. Information about a sta-

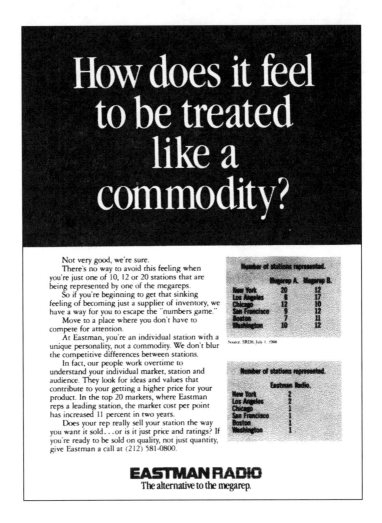

▶ *Figure 2   Rep companies serve a vital sales function for radio stations. Courtesy East-man Radio.*

tion and its market are crucial to the rep. The burden of keeping the rep fully aware of what is happening back at the station rests on the sales manager's shoulders. Since a rep company based in New York or Chicago would have no way of knowing that its client station in West Virginia has decided to carry the local college's football games, it is the station's responsibility to make information available. A rep cannot sell what it doesn't know exists. Of course, a good rep will stay in contact with a station on a regular basis simply to keep abreast of station changes.

There are far fewer radio station reps than there are ad agencies. Approximately 150 reps handle the 9 thousand plus commercial radio stations around the country. Major rep firms, such as Eastman, Blair, and Katz, pitch agencies on behalf of hundreds of client-stations. The larger and very successful reps often refuse to act as the envoy for small market stations because of their lack of earning potential. A rep company typically receives a commission between 5% and 12% on the spot buys made by agencies, and since the national advertising money usually is directed first to the medium and large markets, the bigger commissions are not to be made from handling small market outlets. Many rep companies specialize in small market stations, however.

While a rep company may work agencies on behalf of numerous stations, it will not handle two radio outlets in the same market. Doing so could result in a rep company being placed in the untenable position of competing with itself for a buy, thus creating an obvious conflict of interest.

The majority of station reps provide additional services. In recent years, many have expanded into the area of programming and management consultancy, while almost all offer clients audience research data, as well as aid in developing sales materials such as rate cards.

DIRECT SALES

The subject of direct selling is, the raison d'etre of this little text. Direct sales are the lifeblood of the smaller market radio station, as well as many larger market outlets. WCCO's general sales manager Marc Kalman attests to this. "Quite simply, small and medium size stations depend and live on direct sales." Then why do the least experienced salespeople work exclusively on direct sales, since it is so crucial to the existence of a radio station? First off, let it be understood that everyone on a station's sales staff works the direct/retail category, not just the neophites. Because it is a huge retail world out there, everyone has to be involved in order to cover those vast entrepreneurial reaches. In a small city between 70 and 100 thousand, there is likely to be hundreds, even thousands, of potential radio users, so everyone is required to pitch in. As they say, the business out there seldom comes to you, so you must go to it. It is important to keep in mind that new businesses open everyday, and the station has to be out there to know this.

Beyond the fact that it takes great initiative to reach all the potential business that is out there, why else does a station put its greenest salespeople out on the direct/retail boulevard? To get experience! I can't help recall the important words of my first sales manager, who pointed past his office window to the cityscape and proclaimed

"Son, that's your territory out there. On each one of those streets there's a store or business that you can help and that can help you in return. That's your school down there, and that's your fortune too. Each one of those retailers represents a lesson, a chapter, in the book called radio selling. Some of your instructors are going to be tough task masters. Others will be real helpful and friendly, and a few will be just plain mean and nasty. But each one can teach you something valuable about the profession, and if you're a good student, you'll succeed. Think of each call, each pitch, as the next step toward the realization of your goal. Now get out there and knock 'em dead, and don't come back until you make a sale."

Had I taken my boss's last comment literally, I would not have returned to the station for five weeks. It took me that long to make my first sale. But his advice was bankable. I gained something from my direct involvement with those would-be time purchasers. It was this knowledge that allowed me to make my first close and hundreds thereafter.

Clearly, selling direct constitutes invaluable experience for the fledgling AE. To sell direct you must do it all. To begin with, ferret out the businesses to pitch. Even though there may be thousands of would-be time buyers out there, they have to be located and qualified. Not every type of business is appropriate for every type of radio station. A client has to be *fitted*. This means a *yes* answer to the following question: Is my station, with its particular format, right for this business? A company selling senior citizen housing is probably not going to be helped much by a Top 40 radio station. Sixteen-year-olds don't think much about retirement. Next, develop a plan to make the most out of the money you're asking the client to spend on your station. Then the presentation (pitch) must be made. This is an art and science unto itself and is discussed in Chapter 8. This makes or breaks the call—your career, your life. At least, that's how it seems at the time. If a sale is made (at which time you pledge to that great oversoul of radio salespeople that you will immediately live a more judicious life—a promise quickly forgotten until the next burst of closing euphoria), you must then get the contract into the processing machine and follow through from there. Later (not too much later) the client must be serviced and overdue monies collected. A few months of direct sales involvement will teach you more than all the books ever written about the experience.

Radio is an extraordinary product, so we now direct our attention to what the time-seller sells.

3

▼
▼
▼
▼
▼

The Tangibles of an Intangible

In Chapter 1, we had some fun with the concept of time as the great tangible/intangible. Although radio salespeople sell air-*time*, they do not sell something immaterial or unreal. Quite the reverse, airtime is very real and concrete. It can be heard and its effects documented. Of course, one can't see it or hold it in one's hand. It is certainly true that it is not like any other form of advertising. Newspaper and magazine ads can be cut out by the advertiser and pinned to a bulletin board or taped to a window as tangible evidence of money spent. Television commercials can be seen, but radio commercials are ephemeral sounds flitting through the electromagnetic spectrum with no visual component to help confirm their existence or attest to their reality. However, any informed account executive responds to such terms by stating the simple fact that an effective radio commercial makes a strong and lasting impression in the mind of the listener the same way that a popular song does. "The so-called intangible nature of a radio commercial really only means you can't see it or touch it. There is little doubt, however, that a good spot is concrete and material in its own very unique way. Few of us have gone unaffected or, better still, untouched by radio commercials. If a spot is good, it is felt, and that's a tangible," observes Charles W. Friedman, sales manager, WKVT AM/FM, Brattleboro, Vermont.

Initially considered an experimental or novel way to publicize a product or service, it soon became apparent to advertisers that radio was much more. The results surprised, even amazed, early sponsors who allocated a small portion of their advertising budgets to the new electronic gadget, while pouring the rest into print. Encouraged by radio's performance, advertisers began to invest more heavily. By the 1930s, many prominent companies reallocated substantial portions of their print advertising budgets for radio. These former doubters discovered that radio was a very concrete way to market their products.

Yet the feeling persists to some extent today that radio is an unconventional mode of advertising, especially among small, print-oriented retailers. Usually, the small-market radio station's prime competitor for ad dollars is the local newspaper (although local cable systems have presented nearly as much competition in some areas). Many retailers have used papers for years and perceive radio as a secondary or even frivolous means of advertising. "Retailers who have used print since hanging out their sign are reluctant to change. The toughest factor facing a radio salesperson is the ill-begotten notion that the old way works the best. It is difficult to overcome this kind of mindset," contends Friedman.

Radio is one of the most effective means of advertising ever devised. There is a right way and a wrong way to utilize this extraordinary medium, and the salesperson who knows and understands the unique character of his product is in the strongest position to succeed. To the extent that a radio commercial cannot be held or taped to a cash register, it is intangible. However, the results produced by a carefully conceived campaign can be seen in a cash register. Consistent radio users, from the giant multinational corporations to the so-called mom and poppers, know that a radio commercial can capture people's attention as effectively as anything crossing their field of vision. A 1950s promotional slogan says it best: "Radio gives you more than you can see."

MATERIAL TOOLS

One of the things that helps make radio more tangible to clients are sales materials: media kits that contain rate cards, station profile sheets, feature information, market and audience data, coverage maps, testimonial statements, and so forth. The sales rep uses these materials as reference to her product, as visual aids during presentations, and as drop-offs or handouts to keep the station in front of the client after the call. Figure 3 shows the cover design of a media kit package.

▶ *Figure 3   Media kits contain material designed for client consumption. Courtesy of KFMZ.*

Rate Cards

Rate cards contain information about the cost of advertising on a particular station. Rates for airtime depend on the size of a station's listenership. In other words, the bigger the audience the higher the rates. At the same time, the unit cost of a spot or a feature sponsorship may be effected by the quantity or amount purchased—the bigger the buy the lower the unit price. Also, clients may get discounts for consecutive week purchases over a prescribed period of time (26 or 52 weeks). Figure 4 gives an example of a rate card.

The sales manager and station manager (or owner) work together in formulating the rate card, basing their decisions on ratings (if any) and what the market can support. Chapter 4 discusses in detail the design of rate cards and their applicability to the sales presentation.

98 KFMZ	RATES		Net to Station	
			60s	30s
AAA	5:30 AM - 3 PM Mon-Fri		$35	$33
TAP	5:30 AM - 7 PM Mon-Sat		$30	$28
ROS	Best Time Available (BTA)		$22	$20

	ROS Packages*			
Weekly	25 times		$21	$19
	50 times		$20	$18
Monthly	75 times		$19	$17
	150 times		$18	$16
Annual	300 times		$17	$15
	500 times		$16	$14
	1000 times		$15	$13

* Add $5 for TAP; $10 for AAA.

▶ *Figure 4   Rate cards contain data pertaining to the cost of airtime on a station. Courtesy of KFMZ.*

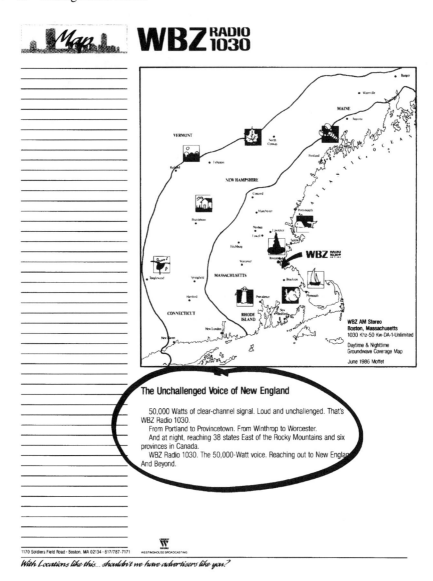

The Unchallenged Voice of New England

50,000 Watts of clear-channel signal. Loud and unchallenged. That's WBZ Radio 1030.
From Portland to Provincetown. From Winthrop to Worcester.
And at night, reaching 38 states East of the Rocky Mountains and six provinces in Canada.
WBZ Radio 1030. The 50,000-Watt voice. Reaching out to New England. And Beyond.

1170 Soldiers Field Road · Boston, MA 02134 · 617/787-7171   WESTINGHOUSE BROADCASTING

With Locations like this... shouldn't we have advertisers like you?

▶ **Figure 5** *If a station has great power and coverage, it wants the client to know. Courtesy WBZ.*

Station Profiles

Station profiles highlight station attributes (strengths) and may focus on an outlet's operating characteristics and personnel. In the former, a station with a super signal and coverage area would want to impress the prospective client with this fact. Take a look at Figure 5. This computes to more potential listeners. Later we look at the function of the coverage map, which is tied to a station's operating parameters and power.

WOOD-AM PROGRAMMING THUMBNAILS

5,000 Watts ● AM Stereo ● 1300 KHZ ● 24 Hours ● NBC

GRAND RAPIDS / WESTERN MICHIGAN COVERAGE AREA

The powerful regional voice of WOOD-AM 1300 blankets Grand Rapids and Western Michigan with an outstanding full service blend of adult contemporary music, entertainment, and information!

GRAND RAPIDS PERSONALITY RADIO

The WOOD-AM 1300 client-oriented air personalities offer you the most influential "sales force" in the region, guaranteeing maximum commercial impact every day! Each of the WOOD personalities are long-time Grand Rapids favorites with a vast adult listener loyalty that will increase your sales.

GRAND RAPIDS MUSIC

WOOD's music is a blend that targets the 35-54 year-old adult, playing the best current releases and the best gold ... all familiar hit music pre-selected to assure consistency and listener enjoyment.

GRAND RAPIDS NEWS / WEATHER

WOOD Radio is Grand Rapids 24-hour news leader! After being honored as "Michigan's News Station of the Year" 3 times in the past 6 years, it's clear that WOOD's award-winning news team is the most complete and professional news force in the Grand Rapids market. The Associated Press News Service, along with the facilities of the NBC Radio Network, further expand the depth and scope of WOOD Radio's journalistic excellence. WOOD Radio's complete weather services department keeps listeners a step ahead with first-hand information from Peter Chan, West Michigan's only full-time radio meteorologist, and WOOD's exclusive Color Weather Radar keeps a 24-hour watch on the weather, so we can tell you well in advance of critical weather situations.

GRAND RAPIDS SPORTS

WOOD-AM 1300 is recognized as the sports leader in the market, programming a heavy schedule of sports scores and highlights in prime drive-time and throughout each day. WOOD-AM carries Detroit Lions football, University of Michigan Wolverines football and basketball, selected Bowl games, the Indy 500 race, the Triple Crown horse races, "live" coverage of the "Gus Macker All World 3-on-3 Basketball Tournament", Football Sunday / Basketball Sunday / Baseball Sunday with Joe Garagiola, Bob Costas' Coast to Coast, and other major sports Tournaments.

WOOD-AM 1300 IS "THE RADIO LEADER" IN GRAND RAPIDS

News, Weather, Traffic, Sports, TalkNet with Bruce Williams, The Larry King Show, Farm Information, Entertainment, plus a dedication to Local Public Service Events round out the WOOD-AM programming philosophy. WOOD-AM 1300 is "The Radio Leader", offering you the very best in full service Adult Contemporary / Personality radio!

▶ *Figure 6*   *A quick survey of a station's offerings. Courtesy of WOOD.*

Stations also publish capsule (thumbnail) profiles that highlight their key offerings. Most general station profiles include a statement about power and operating hours, top personalities, and formatics (music aired, news, sports, and weather presentations, and special programming). Examine the profile sheet in Figure 6.

Many stations market their air personalities, because these individuals gain celebrity status in the community. This makes them salable and enhances the station's appeal for a prospective sponsor. Popular radio personalities make stations a lot of money, so personality profile sheets are an integral part of station media kits. About 80% of station media kits include personality profiles, such as the one in

★CAROLE ☆HEMINGWAY:

For eight years Carole Hemingway reigned as Los Angeles' top nightime talk personality, originating the investigative talk radio format.

In 1984 and 1985 she hosted the "Carole Hemingway Show" on WABC, New York, and the national PBS television "Latenight America." Now, Hemingway shares her special talents with KGIL's daytime listeners in L.A.'s most enticing talk radio program.

Hemingway has interviewed thousands, including the world's leading celebrities. Critically. Candidly. Compassionately.

From Richard Nixon to Michael Jackson, Natalie Wood to Menachem Begin –

Hemingway captures the private side of the public figure. Elected "Woman of the Year" by the City of Hope, Hemingway was also honored with the first Susan B. Anthony Award for outstanding journalism, and received a Golden Mike for a documentary on the Middle East. The City of Los Angeles proclaimed Carole Hemingway Day in tribute to her deep belief in human rights.

The Hemingway Touch: It's provoking. Enlightening. And Entertaining.

CAROLE HEMINGWAY:

ANOTHER REASON TO LISTEN TO KGIL-AM/1260

▶ *Figure 7*   *Stations sell their stars. Courtesy of KGIL.*

Figure 7. What most station personality profile sheets share in common is a desire to portray their popular air people as informative, entertaining, and human (real people despite their extraordinary gifts).

Feature Sheets

A media kit or sales packet includes write-ups devoted to important station programming features. Features are a primary motivator for advertisers, so a sales packet includes them. While some stations are very feature-oriented, especially full-service stations, others offer very few. This obviously has a bearing on the density of a station's kit. I received a station media kit that contained no less than two dozen different feature sheets. Figure 8 shows two examples of feature sheets.

Note that in Figure 8b the station has indicated the cost of sponsorship. Not only will stations include general info feature sheets in kits, but they often include sheets promoting purchasable station features.

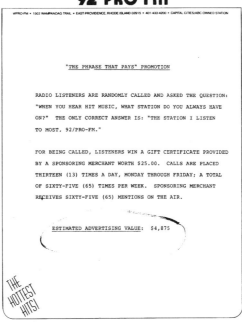

▶ *Figure 8(a and b)* *Feature sheets such as these visualize station offerings for sponsors.*
Courtesy of WOOD and WPRO.

Audience Data

One of the goals of a station sales rep is to convince a potential sponsor of his station's effectiveness in reaching the buying public, in particular that segment of the listening public that wants or needs a sponsor's product or service. Media kits include marketing and audience data sheets to assist in this effort.

Observe what information the audience sheets convey in Figure 9 a–c. Certainly, a prospective advertiser would find interesting the information KCS includes in its media kit. For instance, if you were considering investing your business's hard earned dollars in a spot scheduled on this station it would be reassuring to know that it has listener loyalty, reaches your important buying demographic, and is on the air around-the-clock. It is certainly not a bad idea to include such information in a sales packet.

The audience information in some packets can be elaborate, as provided by WOOD and KFMZ. Data may include comprehensive studies that pertain to area economics and lifestyles. This information can be useful, because would-be advertisers are quite interested in just how a station fits in with all of this.

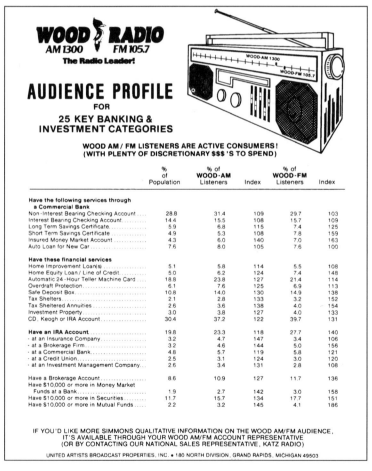

WOOD RADIO
AM 1300   FM 105.7
The Radio Leader!

AUDIENCE PROFILE
FOR
**25 KEY BANKING &
INVESTMENT CATEGORIES**

WOOD AM / FM LISTENERS ARE ACTIVE CONSUMERS!
(WITH PLENTY OF DISCRETIONARY $$$ 'S TO SPEND)

	% of Population	% of WOOD-AM Listeners	Index	% of WOOD-FM Listeners	Index
Have the following services through a Commercial Bank					
Non-Interest Bearing Checking Account	28.8	31.4	109	29.7	103
Interest Bearing Checking Account	14.4	15.5	108	15.7	109
Long Term Savings Certificate	5.9	6.8	115	7.4	125
Short Term Savings Certificate	4.9	5.3	108	7.8	159
Insured Money Market Account	4.3	6.0	140	7.0	163
Auto Loan for New Car	7.6	8.0	105	7.6	100
Have these financial services					
Home Improvement Loan(s)	5.1	5.8	114	5.5	108
Home Equity Loan / Line of Credit	5.0	6.2	124	7.4	148
Automatic 24 - Hour Teller Machine Card	18.8	23.8	127	21.4	114
Overdraft Protection	6.1	7.6	125	6.9	113
Safe Deposit Box	10.8	14.0	130	14.9	138
Tax Shelters	2.1	2.8	133	3.2	152
Tax Sheltered Annuities	2.6	3.6	138	4.0	154
Investment Property	3.0	3.8	127	4.0	133
CD, Keogh or IRA Account	30.4	37.2	122	39.7	131
Have an IRA Account	19.8	23.3	118	27.7	140
- at an Insurance Company	3.2	4.7	147	3.4	106
- at a Brokerage Firm	3.2	4.6	144	5.0	156
- at a Commercial Bank	4.8	5.7	119	5.8	121
- at a Credit Union	2.5	3.1	124	3.0	120
- at an Investment Management Company	2.6	3.4	131	2.8	108
Have a Brokerage Account	8.6	10.9	127	11.7	136
Have $10,000 or more in Money Market Funds at a Bank	1.9	2.7	142	3.0	158
Have $10,000 or more in Securities	11.7	15.7	134	17.7	151
Have $10,000 or more in Mutual Funds	2.2	3.2	145	4.1	186

IF YOU'D LIKE MORE SIMMONS QUALITATIVE INFORMATION ON THE WOOD AM/FM AUDIENCE,
IT'S AVAILABLE THROUGH YOUR WOOD AM/FM ACCOUNT REPRESENTATIVE
(OR BY CONTACTING OUR NATIONAL SALES REPRESENTATIVE, KATZ RADIO)

UNITED ARTISTS BROADCAST PROPERTIES, INC. • 180 NORTH DIVISION, GRAND RAPIDS, MICHIGAN 49503

a

▶ *Figure 9a-c   Published audience data are useful in convincing sponsors of a station's effectiveness. Courtesy of WOOD, KFMZ, and KCS.*

Retail Buying Power

Retail Sales

Total Retail Sales	592,121,000
Food Stores	119,115,000
Supermarkets	116,906,000
Eating & Drinking Places	60,316,000
General Merchandise Stores	90,661,000
Department Stores	86,784,000
Apparel & Accessories Stores	36,325,000
Automotive Dealers	142,883,000
Building Materials & Hardware	35,614,000
Drug Stores	15,746,000
Furniture & Appliance Stores	10,863,000
Radio, TV & Music Stores	8,049,000

Columbia's Effective Buying Income

Total Effective Buying Income	1,454,111,000
Effective Buying Income Per Household	36,944
Median Buying Income	27,353
Retail Expenditures Per Household	14,840

Population Breakdown

Total (12+)		95,000
12-17	7.5%	7,100
18-34	52.0%	49,400
35-49	19.9%	18,900
50+	20.6%	19,600
Median Age: 25.0 Years		

Household Income Breakdown

Total Household		40,600
Under $10,000	15.5%	6,285
10-19,999	21.6%	8,767
20-29,999	17.6%	7,137
30-39,999	13.3%	5,406
40-49,999	10.8%	4,395
50,000+	21.2%	8,610

Source: Marketing Statistics, Sales and Marketing Management's 1988 "Survey of Buying Power."

b

P.O. BOX 1345 ▲ 1101 EAST WALNUT ▲ COLUMBIA, MO 65205
314-874-3000 ▲ FAX 314-443-1460

KCS LISTENER PROFILE

EXCLUSIVITY:
Over 50% of the entire KCS audience listen exclusively to KCS, Monday through Friday.

SUPERBUYERS:
Over 60% of KCS listeners are age 25-54, the "Superbuyers" in their peak years of acquisition, with discretionary incomes to ring your cash register.

LOYALTY:
KCS listeners stay tuned longer, almost two hours each day, with less turnover in audience than virtually any other station in Colorado Springs. Since 1978, KCS has enjoyed high listener loyalty because KCS gives the audience what it wants: more country music with less talk.

LISTENING LOCATIONS:
People listen to KCS everywhere. Men listen equally at home, at work, and in their cars. Over 1/2 of all KCS women listen at home while nearly 1/3 listen in their cars.

KCS--ROUND THE CLOCK:
KCS leads the market in overnight listening.

Source: Arbitron

KCS delivers an upscale audience that's unequaled in responsible adults with discretionary incomes, good jobs, homes and families. They are extremely loyal to KCS and have been for over a decade. And they listen, almost exclusively to KCS, at all hours of the day and night, at home, at work, while traveling and having fun. They count on KCS to be there today and tomorrow, with no surprises. KCS listeners respond with their hearts, their hands, their heads, their loyalty and their money!

c

▶ *Figure 9* continued.

Coverage Maps

These are the Rand McNally's of a station's reach. Obviously, the potency of a station's signal is a topic of interest to someone about to invest advertising dollars. To satisfy this need to know, stations invariably include coverage maps in their media kits. Some are very basic, whereas others can be very elaborate. Notice WOOD's coverage map in Figure 10. What important points would you note to a retail client in the town of Rockford? For starters, her business exists in the very heart of the station's signal. The most shaded area of the map shows the fullest signal strength. That's good because everybody within at least a 30-mile radius can hear the station loud and clear. Since WOOD-FM is located a few miles away in the city of Grand Rapids, the client's spots will benefit from being at the epicenter of the station's area of dominant influent (ADI). Buying on WOOD has a double advantage for this particular retailer since she is about to open another store in Lowell, just south of Grand Rapids. Because of its location, it will enjoy the same signal benefits as the store in Rockford. Clients can easily relate to the information in a coverage map, because it is clear and accessible, unlike the sophisticated information that often exists in marketing charts and graphs. This coverage map instantly relates these important facts to the client:

1. WOOD's signal covers half of the state.

2. A third of the state is in the station's ADI.

3. WOOD is one of the most powerful station's around.

4. WOODs programming can be tuned in most of the state's largest cities.

5. The potential audience is in the millions.

All of this is important to convey to the retailer, because this client is opening stores in locations covered very effectively by the station's powerful signal.

Testimonials

It's your job to say great things about the station you work for. Imagine the effects of this kind of statement on a prospective sponsor:

> "Well, we do a pretty fair job considering the fact that we're a low-power AM daytimer. Of course, this time of year we go off the air around 4 o'clock, so we lose the afternoon commuter audience, and do you have any idea just how difficult it is to get listeners back once they tune another station? It doesn't help either that most music listeners tune FM and that we're one of four adult music stations in this economically depressed market. So, you want to sign on? We're the station for you!"

The competition should send this person a check. The point is, no one expects a sales rep to say anything but wonderful things about his station, so client testimonials carry weight. These people are cut from the same entrepreneurial cloth; they are brothers and sisters in the retail army, out to make a living and hopefully generate business by advertising on the radio. When they have succeeded and convey why, and your station is part of the why, this is a valuable tool in helping convince

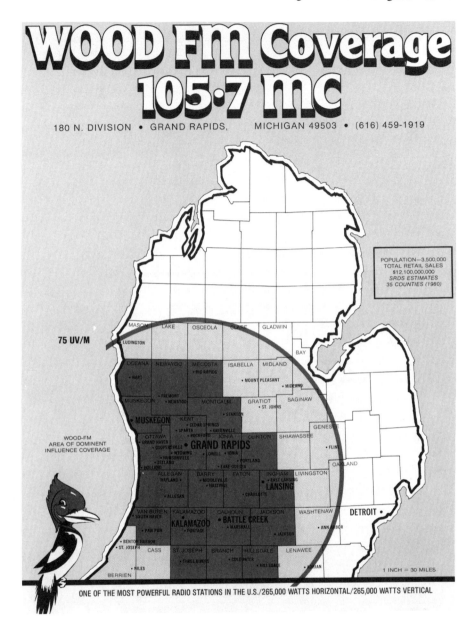

▶ *Figure 10*   *Coverage maps illustrate a station's reach. Courtesy WOOD.*

others to buy. Testimonials from fellow business people carry a kind of credibility a salesperson does not, and a statement corroborating your claims can be a real boost. All sponsors like a little assurance that their decision is a smart one, and testimony from other advertisers is positive proof that the station delivers on its promises (see Figure 11).

R & D LABS

5010 Sunset Boulevard
Los Angeles, CA 90027
(213) 668-1922

Ms. Lois Garon
% KGIL RADIO
14800 Lassen
Mission Hills, CA   91345

Dear Lois,

Did you know you have a very responsive listening audience who are truely interested in staying healthy using nutrition?

The Monday after the show aired on the Reams Body Chemistry Analysis, we had several calls and bookings for appointments, and as the week progressed the phone just kept ringing. Some of the callers were long time listeners, and others just tuned in and stayed with us for the rest of the show.

This has been one of the most successful radio shows we have done in L.A. County, and I just wanted you to know what an impact your show is making on the community.

From our previous experience I know we will continue to get calls in the next few weeks, but if no one else called, we would consider this a great success.

Thanks so very much for your excellent and timely interview, and for your support of our cause.

Cordially,

Kaye Champagne
Executive Director

Nutritional Testing   Colon Hydrotherapy   Nutritional Consulting & Courses

▶ *Figure 11   Testimonial letters corroborate the AEs claims. Courtesy KGIL.*

Stations usually solicit testimonial letters from satisfied sponsors for use in sales packets. In fact, some stations routinely collect testimonials from every type of account. Think how useful a testimonial letter would be by a jewelry store advertiser when you were pitching another jewelry store. If the jewelry store offering the testimonial is currently on the air, great. There is no problem concerning competition. There's room for everybody on a station that pumps a signal into the ether around-the-clock, year-round.

Promotional Bric-à-Brac

Included in many media kit packets are promo freebees, such as pens, bumper stickers, buttons, magnets, and balloons. Let's face it, it's a hoot to get something for free, even a pen with station call letters on it. The idea behind these little gifts is to give the client something and keep the station visible after the sales rep is gone.

> "If you'd please give me your signature right here with your spiffy new, and I might add one-of-a-kind, ball-point pen, you'll become an official member of the X109 'Pen Pal' family. Oh, and please don't forget to wear your 'X marks the spot' happy face button and 'X-me on the lips' painter's cap."

Well, you get the idea. Promotional paraphernalia have a real (tangible) value. They are by no means throwaway stuff. At the very least, they serve to remind the world of the station's existence—a pretty inexpensive form of station advertising. (Ah, the deceit!) You sign a sponsor to get her advertising dollars on your station, then load her down with call letter emblazened doodads to promote your station. (Not deceitful—ingenious.)

USING MATERIALS

Media kits do not sell a client, but they can certainly aid in this objective. Promotional materials say a lot about a station. They reveal it. They help make a station more real. Broadcasters may begrudgingly admit this, but printed information carries the weight of legitimacy. Each item in a packet should inspire a positive impression of a station and should give a strong overview of what the AE has to offer.

There is a right way and not so right way to use visuals, if you will. Again, do not assume they alone can sell a client. You have to work them, choreograph them to achieve the effect you are after. A good salesperson doesn't work directly out of a kit, but rather integrates aspects of it into her presentation. Select in advance what parts of the packet you'll employ. During a presentation, don't dig through your pouch of materials like a circus clown does his bottomless, gag-filled satchel. You'll look just as silly.

A sales kit should not be regarded as a handout. Rather, it should be used as an integral part of your presentation. For example, bring out a profile sheet when you're giving an overview of the station. Use the coverage map to impress the client with the station's potential audience. Draw on audience data as it pertains to your sell. This holds true for program and personality sheets, testimonials, and other ingredients of the packet. A mistake many salespeople make is to regard this material cavalierly and casually say, "Take a look at this when you get a chance." Forget it! Retailers seldom invest time and energy reading media kits. In other words, use station materials to your advantage while you're face-to-face with the client.

There's nothing wrong with leaving materials behind once the in-person presentation has been made, but tailor the kit to suit the call. That is, don't leave the client with everything the station has ever printed about itself. Thin it down. Make it lean and mean. For example, if you have just called on the Bel Air Diner on route 9, leave a kit containing your coverage map (that shows your signal reaches a 5-state area) and audience data sheet (showing how more car radios are tuned to your station than any other) that means travelers are likely to hear about the Bel Air's super highway meatloaf special. Bottom line, make everything you do relevant to the business that you are attempting to put on the air.

One last thing, some stations do not want rate cards left behind for a couple of reasons (1) the client seldom knows how to adequately interpret it, and this can lead to confusion and frustration; and (2) a station may not want its rates publicized, especially for the benefit of the competition. Obviously, if a client requests that a rate card be left behind, a refusal can make for awkwardness. If it is the station's policy not to leave a rate card with a client, just make it clear from the start through gestures and body language (before words) that the one you are using is the only one you have as your personal work sheet. Make certain you know what your station's policy is on this score. Go ahead, talk to your sales manager. Don't forget, you're in a business whose stock in trade is communication.

WRITTEN PRESENTATIONS

Written presentations are intended to provide a prospective client with a carefully tailored plan to increase business through using station airtime. When they are done thoughtfully, they can be very effective in helping persuade a retailer to use radio as an advertising medium.

Written presentations convey a number of things to a prospective sponsor. They show that an AE cares enough to spend the time and energy required to put on paper a plan that is based on the realities of a client's business. A good written presentation shows that you're a pro at what you do, and people respect a pro. This communicates to the prospective advertiser that they are dealing with someone who is informed and knowledgeable. Written presentations foster credibility and confidence.

In an ideal world a written presentation would be composed for every prospective client. However, a well prepared paper presentation takes time, and time is a very precious commodity to a direct-retail account person. Therefore, written presentations are typically prepared for hard-to-sell clients, larger enterprises, and heavy media users. Dealing with the aforementioned requires formidable ammunition.

The idea behind a written presentation is to give the client a highly targeted and super-relevant plan designed to generate business through the use of your radio station. Therefore, observe the following steps during the preparation of a written proposal:

1. Get a close-up view of what the business is all about. You must learn everything possible about the client's product or service. If the client owns a retail outlet, make a visit; assume the role of a customer. A clear picture of the store's look, location, merchandise, and clientele is absolutely necessary.

2. Make an assessment of the area (town) in which the business operates. Who lives in the area and what are they like, demographically speaking? This helps give you an idea of the store's traffic potential.

3. Undertake an evaluation of the store's location. How does it enhance or discourage customer traffic. A bad location is something that must be considered in any plan designed to improve business.

4. Review the product inventory. What the store sells is an important factor in how to sell the store.

5. Conduct a study of competitive businesses. Their impact on the client must be assessed.

6. Engage in an analysis of prior and current advertising efforts. Has the client used radio or other media before, and how effectively?

These are just a few of the things that inform a presentation.

Once the homework has been done, the salesperson is in a position to compose a proposal that makes sense to the client. An obvious example, of an appropriate proposal, would be to tie in a sporting goods store with a station sports feature. That doesn't require genius level thinking, but orchestrating the presentation is both intellectually and emotionally challenging. The obvious often needs to be hunted. Don't automatically assume that because a store sells basketballs they'd love to sponsor a station's high-school games. It generally takes more to convince a client that this is a smart decision, and that is what a carefully prepared written presentation is all about. Document your claims in a manner that will force the client to acknowledge the wisdom in your offer. Keep in mind that you are making an offer.

A written proposal should contain a *title page* (with the client's name in bold print), the station's call letters, and the name of the sales rep; a *contents page* (an outline of what is included in the proposal); the *proposal/plan* itself (what and how much); *selected material* from the station's media kit (a feature/personality profile, etc.) as pertains to the plan; and last, but not least, a fully prepared *contract* (consistent with the plan).

Keep the presentation clear and client-friendly. Avoid industry jargon. Don't assume the client understands terms like daypart, bulk plan, availabilities, flights, BTA, and so on. Spell things out. Ambiguity constitutes a boulder on the path to a sale. Use plain English, people talk. A written sales presentation doesn't have to be a work of literature, but it should not look like something thrown together. It is a reflection of you and your station. Proofread it to eliminate spelling and punctuation errors and typos. Have someone else read it if you're not a world-class grammarian.

Of course, keep in mind that a written presentation alone seldom inspires a buy on the direct-retail level. As the saying goes, "You've got to put the body behind the proposal."

4

Rate Cards, Features, and Packages

The fees that stations charge sponsors for airtime are published in rate cards and feature plans. Clearly, salespeople must be adept at using rate cards. A lack of familiarity with what a station charges for its commercial airtime can spell disaster. The first thing a new salesperson must master is the station's rate structure. A salesperson who doesn't know what his product costs can't do anyone any good, for example:

"So, if your commercials are heard on 'Berry's Bandstand,' you'll be reaching the audience who uses and buys your product."

"Okay, let's give it a try. How much is a 60-second commercial on the 'Bandstand' show?"

"Just a second. Let me see. Somewhere between $8 and $14... I think."

Not a good way to instill confidence in a client. Sure, this is an extreme example of rate card ignorance, but there should be no mystery at all when it comes to your station's rate card.

THE RATE CARD

Rates for airtime depend upon the size of a station's listenership. That is, the bigger the audience the higher the rates and the demand for availabilities. At the same time, the unit cost for a spot or a feature may be affected by the quantity or amount purchased: the bigger the buy, the cheaper the unit price. Clients may also get discounts for consecutive week purchases over a prescribed period of time, say 26 or 52 weeks. There are stations that sell only at a fixed rate, meaning no discounts. The rate remains the same regardless of quantity of purchase or calendar.

INGREDIENTS OF THE RATE CARD

Policy Statements

The sales manager and station manager collaborate on the design of the rate card, basing their decisions on ratings and what the market will support. A typical rate card includes a brief *policy* statement concerning terms of payment and commission.

Subject to conditions in X109 agreement form with specific additions/ substitutions noted, binding when executed by station management. Invoices payable on or before the 10th of the month following broadcast. Invoices subject to finance and collection charges. Rate subject to change without advance notice. Station reserves the right to reject, refuse or discontinue any contract for reasons satisfactory to itself. Without prior credit approval, cash in advance required. Commission to recognized advertising agencies on net charges for station—15%.

A statement pertaining to the nature of copy, when it is due at the station, and hourly spot load limits also may be included in the rate card.

All programs and announcements are subject to removal without notice for any broadcast that, in our opinion, is not in the public's interest. Copy must be at the station 48 hours prior to broadcast date and before noon on days preceding weekends and holidays. Maximum of 10 minutes of commercials per hour. X109 recommends not more than one commercial per advertiser, per hour for maximum listenership and exposure.

A station's approach to discounting must, of practical necessity, be included in the card.

"All programs, features, and announcements are provided a 5% discount if on the air for 26 consecutive weeks and a 10% discount if on the air for one year or longer."

It is incumbent on an AE to be thoroughly familiar with policy stated in the station's rate card. Policy is not written to be ignored. Read up! (see Figure 12.)

It is important to state as emphatically and clearly as possible the station's position on all possible topics affecting a sale. Most stations provide clients rate protection for a designated period of time should fees for airtime change (a shifting of grids for example). This means that if a client purchases a 3-month spot schedule in June, and the station ups its rates in July, the advertiser continues to pay the original rates until the expiration of its current contract.

The rate card also contains its feature and spot rates. Among the most prevalent features that stations offer are traffic, sports, weather, and business (stock) reports. Newscasts also are available to advertisers. Features generally include an open (introduction) and a 30- or 60-second announcement. They are particularly effective advertising vehicles because listeners tend to pay greater attention. Conditions pertaining to feature buys usually appear in the rate card: "All feature sales are subject to 4-weeks notice for renewal and cancellation." A station wants to establish credibility with its features and therefore prefers to maintain continuity among its sponsors. A feature with a regular sponsor conveys stability, and that is what a station seeks.

CARD # 34   8/1/89
Net to Station

98 KFMZ

RATES

		60s	30s
AAA	5:30 AM - 3 PM Mon-Fri	$35	$33
TAP	5:30 AM - 7 PM Mon-Sat	$30	$28
ROS	Best Time Available (BTA)	$22	$20

ROS Packages*

Weekly	25 times	$21	$19
	50 times	$20	$18
Monthly	75 times	$19	$17
	150 times	$18	$16
Annual	300 times	$17	$15
	500 times	$16	$14
	1000 times	$15	$13

* Add $5 for TAP; $10 for AAA.

a

MAGIC 94.3
IN THE VALLEY   KMGX FM

TOTAL AUDIENCE PACKAGE	GRIDS Rates are for 1 minute or less				
5-day Minimum, 7-Day Maximum, 2:1 Ratio	I	II	III	IV	V
6 am - 8 pm (2/3)	70	60	50	45	40
8 pm - 12 Mid (1/3)	60	50	40	35	30
FIXED DAYPARTS MON - FRI 6 am - 10 am & 3 pm - 8 pm	85	75	65	60	55
10 am - 3 pm	75	65	55	50	45
8 pm - 12 Mid	60	50	40	35	30
SATURDAY & SUNDAY 6 am - 12 Mid	55	50	45	35	30

b

Rates for newscasts, features, and remote broadcasts on request.
All rates quoted are valid for 10 days.

▶ *Figure 12a-f   Rate cards usually stipulate the conditions of the buy. Courtesy KFMZ, KMGX, KCS, WDSD, and WOOD.*

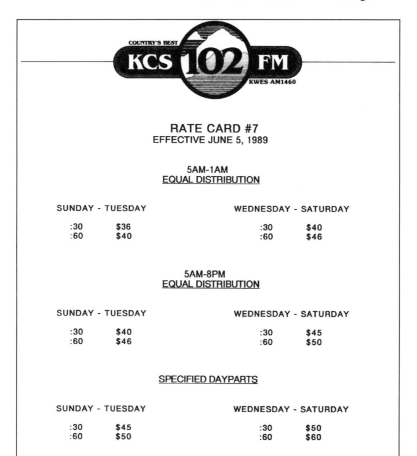

▶ *Figure 12   continued.*

"Rate cards may be revised infrequently or too frequently—the latter may create an image of instability from the perspective of the time buyer. Usually, cards are dated and numbered and revised as the fate of the station (ratings) or economy (recession) changes. Some rate cards, especially those employing the grid structure, stipulate seasonal adjustments in rates."

Grids

Many stations use a grid structure. This gives stations a considerable degree of rate flexibility. For example, if a station has five rate-level grids, it may have a range of between $20 and $50 for a 60-second spot. Clients would then be given rates at

WDOV-WDSD COMBINATION RATE CARD

Effective October 1988

		GRID I	GRID II	GRID III	GRID IV	GRID V
FIXED POSITION:						
	:30	$52.00	$44.00	$40.00	$35.00	$32.00
	:60	$64.00	$54.00	$48.00	$42.00	$39.00
PLAN I:	5 am - 8 pm					
	:30	$44.00	$36.00	$32.00	$28.00	$26.00
	:60	$54.00	$44.00	$39.00	$34.00	$31.00
PLAN II	5 am - 11 pm					
	:30	$42.00	$34.00	$30.00	$26.00	$24.00
	:60	$52.00	$41.00	$36.00	$31.00	$29.00

P.O. DRAWER B • DOVER, DELAWARE 19903
302-674-1410 • 302-734-5816 • FAX 302-674-8621

d

▶ *Figure 12   continued.*

the lower grid if the station had few sponsors on the air, thus creating many avail-abilities (places to insert commercial messages). As business increased at the station and availabilities became scarcer, the station would then ask for rates reflected in the upper grids. Gridding is based upon the age-old concept of supply and demand. When availabilities are tight, airtime is at a premium; it costs more.

 **AM/FM COMBO PROGRAM SPONSORSHIPS**

DRIVETIME TRAFFIC REPORTS (Direct from the Grand Rapids Police Department)
Monday - Friday rotation . . . 6:45 a.m., 7:15 a.m., 7:45 a.m., 8:15 a.m., 3:45 p.m.*, 4:15 p.m.*, 4:45 p.m.*, 5:15 p.m.*
*3:45 through 5:15 p.m. reports air on WOOD-AM only, and a matching commercial will air on WOOD-FM between 3:30 and 5:30 p.m.
Includes opening billboard mention, plus :60-second commercial.

OPEN GRID RATES:			YEARLY CONTRACT RATES:			
I	II	III	125x	250x	500x	750x
$135	$130	$125	$120	$115	$110	$105

DRIVETIME WEATHER FORECASTS
Monday - Saturday rotation . . . 5:56 a.m., 6:56 a.m., 7:56 a.m., 8:56 a.m., 3:56 p.m.*, 4:56 p.m.*, 5:56 p.m.*

3:56 through 5:56 p.m. forecasts air on WOOD-AM only, and a matching commercial will air on WOOD-FM between 4:00 and 6:00 p.m.
*Monday - Friday only
Includes opening billboard mention, plus :60-second commercial.

OPEN GRID RATES:			YEARLY CONTRACT RATES:			
I	II	III	125x	250x	500x	750x
$120	$115	$110	$105	$100	$ 95	$ 90

DRIVETIME SPORTSCASTS
Monday - Saturday rotation . . . 5:33 a.m.*, 6:20 a.m., 7:20 a.m., 8:20 a.m., 4:20 p.m.*, 5:20 p.m.*, 6:20 p.m.*
4:20 through 6:20 p.m. sportscasts air on WOOD-AM only, and a matching commercial will air on WOOD-FM between 4:30 and 6:30 p.m.
*Monday - Friday only
Includes opening billboard mention, plus :60-second commercial.

OPEN GRID RATES:			YEARLY CONTRACT RATES:			
I	II	III	125x	250x	500x	750x
$115	$110	$105	$100	$ 95	$ 90	$ 85

ROTATING NEWSCASTS (featuring WOOD's award-winning News Team)
Monday - Saturday rotation
On WOOD-AM: 5:03 a.m., 5:30 a.m., 6:03 a.m., 6:30 a.m., 7:03 a.m., 7:30 a.m., 8:03 a.m., 8:30 a.m., 9:03 a.m.,
10:03 a.m., 11:03 a.m., 12:03 p.m., 1:03 p.m., 2:03 p.m., 3:03 p.m., 4:03 p.m., 5:03 p.m.,
6:03 p.m., 7:03 p.m.*, 8:03 p.m.*, 9:03 p.m.*, 10:03 p.m.*   *Monday - Friday only

On WOOD-FM: 5:30 a.m., 6:03 a.m., 6:30 a.m., 7:03 a.m., 7:30 a.m., 8:03 a.m., 8:30 a.m., 9:00 a.m., 9:57 a.m.,
10:57 a.m., 11:57 a.m., 12:57 p.m., 1:57 p.m., 2:57 p.m., 3:57 p.m., 4:57 p.m., 5:57 p.m.,
6:57 p.m., 7:57 p.m., 8:57 p.m., 9:57 p.m.

Includes two sponsor name mentions, plus :60-second commercial.

OPEN GRID RATES:			YEARLY CONTRACT RATES:			
I	II	III	125x	250x	500x	750x
$110	$105	$100	$ 95	$ 90	$ 85	$ 80

GENERAL INFORMATION

FACILITIES:
WOOD-AM 5,000 watts, fulltime, stereo, directional evenings   WOOD-FM 265,000 watts, fulltime, stereo
COPY DEADLINES:
A. Copy to be written by station must be received by Noon, two (2) working days prior to broadcast.
B. Agency copy delivery is the responsibility of agency and must be in the station by 12 Noon the working day prior to broadcast.
C. One minute – 150 words maximum; 30-second – 75 words maximum.
RATE POLICIES:
A. Billing monthly, payable within 30 days with approved credit.
B. Short term broadcasting, promotion/special events, payable in advance.
C. Political broadcasting rates upon request; terms: net cash payment in advance, 48 hours closing.

e

▶ *Figure 12 continued.*

Grids are inventory sensitive. They allow a station to remain viable when business is at a low ebb. Certainly when inventory prices reach a bargain level this encourages business. For instance, during a period when advertiser activity is sluggish, a station that can offer spots at a considerable reduction stands a chance of stimulating buyer interest.

AM/FM COMBO RATE CARD 4C
EFFECTIVE NOVEMBER 13, 1989

	Open Grid Rates		I	II	III
TAP I	:60		$125	$120	$115
	:30		$112	S108	$104
1/3 5:30 a.m. - 10:00 a.m.	**Yearly Contract Rates**	125x	250x	500x	750x
1/3 10:00 a.m. - 3:00 p.m.	:60	$110	$105	$100	$ 95
1/3 3:00 p.m. - 8:00 p.m.	:30	$ 99	$ 94	$ 90	$ 86

	Open Grid Rates		I	II	III
TAP II	:60		$110	$105	$100
	:30		$ 99	$ 94	$ 90
1/4 5:30 a.m. - 10:00 a.m.					
1/4 10:00 a.m. - 3:00 p.m	**Yearly Contract Rates**	125x	250x	500x	750x
1/4 3:00 p.m. - 8:00 p.m.	:60	$ 95	$ 90	$ 85	$ 80
1/4 8:00 p.m. - 12 mid. and/or	:30	$ 86	$ 81	$ 76	$ 72
Sun. 8:00 a.m. - 12 mid.					

	Open Grid Rates		I	II	III
TAP III	:60		$ 95	$ 90	$ 85
	:30		$ 86	$ 81	$ 76
1/5 5:30 a.m. - 10:00 a.m.					
1/5 10:00 a.m. - 3:00 p.m.					
1/5 3:00 p.m. - 8:00 p.m.	**Yearly Contract Rates**	125x	250x	500x	750x
1/5 8:00 p.m. - 12 mid. and/or	:60	$ 80	$ 75	$ 70	$ 65
Sun. 8:00 a.m. - 12 mid.	:30	$ 72	$ 67	$ 63	$ 59
1/5 12 mid. - 5:30 a.m.					

6-DAY DISCOUNT	Deduct $10 for TAP Plan schedules rotating on 6 of 7 consecutive days. 1/6 of the schedule must air on Saturday and/or Sunday.
WEEKEND/EVENING PACKAGE	Saturday 5:30 - 10:00 a.m., 10:00 a.m. - 3:00 p.m., 3:00 - 8:00 p.m., 8:00 p.m. - 12 mid. Sunday 11:00 a.m. - 3:00 p.m., 3:00 - 8:00 p.m., 8:00 p.m. - 12 mid. Monday-Friday 8:00 p.m. - 12 mid. No more than one-half of the weekly commercials may air Saturday 10:00 a.m. - 3:00 p.m. Flat $58 rate for :60's or :30's.
DAYPART RATES	Monday-Friday 5:30 - 10:00 a.m. Add $20 to applicable TAP I rate Monday-Friday 10:00 a.m. - 3:00 p.m. . . . . Subtract $20 from applicable TAP I rate Monday-Friday 3:00 - 8:00 p.m. . . . . Use applicable TAP I rate "10:00 a.m. - 3:00 p.m. Package" . . . . Flat $68 rate with purchase of 10x or more per week.
OVERNIGHT SPECIAL	Advertisers may purchase Overnight Commercials for 10% of their applicable TAP or daypart rate. These commercials will be aired on a full 12 midnight - 5:30 a.m. rotation.
ON-LOCATION BROADCASTS	Rates available upon request.

f

▶ *Figure 12* *continued.*

Meanwhile, when business is brisk at a station, due to holiday buying for example, then the situation may be exploited in a manner positive to the revenue column. Again, the supply and demand concept at work (the idea upon which capitalism is based).

Again, not all stations grid their rate cards. However, since the late 1970s, this system has gained considerable popularity because of its relevance to the ever fluctuating economy. As apparent in the rate cards exhibited in the chapter, grids are delineated by some sort of scale, usually alphabetical or numerical.

Dayparting

Since the size of a station's audience generally varies depending on the time of day, rates for spots and features must reflect that fact. Thus, the broadcast day is divided into time zones or classifications. A station's prime selling period is typically 6:00–10:00 A.M. weekdays and therefore may be designated as *AAA* (triple A), while afternoon drivetime, usually 3:00–7:00 P.M., may be called *AA* (double A) because of its secondary drawing power. Under this system, the midday segment, 10:00 A.M.–3:00 P.M., would be given an *A* (single A) designation, and evenings, 7:00 P.M.–12:00 A.M., a *B*. Overnights, 12:00 A.M.–6:00 A.M., may be classified as *C* time. Obviously the fees charged for spots are established on an ascending scale from *C–AAA*. A station may charge $300 for an announcement aired at 8:00 A.M. and $45 for one aired at 2:00 A.M. The difference in the size of the station's audience at those hours warrants the contrast.

There are variations of the preceding approach. Some stations do not daypart this extensively, preferring to charge a fixed rate throughout the day for a 60 or 30, and perhaps a different (reduced) rate during late evening hours. Clients who buy schedules during a specific daypart see their spots rotated within that time frame.

DISCOUNTING

As already mentioned, the more airtime a client purchases, the less expensive the cost for an individual commercial (unit) at many stations. For instance, if an advertiser buys 12 spots a week in Triple A time, the cost of each spot would be slightly less than if the sponsor purchased just 2 spots a week. A client must buy a specific number of spots in order to benefit from a frequency discount. A 6X rate, meaning 6 spots per week, for *AAA* 60s (60-second announcement) may be $75 per spot, while the 12X rate may be $71 and the 18X rate $68, and so forth. A 30-second spot usually is priced at two-thirds the cost of a 60. Should a client desire that a spot be aired at a fixed time, say 7:10 A.M. daily, the station will tack on an additional charge, possibly 20%. Fixed position drive-time spots are among the most expensive in a station's inventory.

BTA/ROS

Clients can choose several spot schedules suited for their advertising and budgetary needs. For advertisers with limited funds, run-of-station/schedule (ROS) or best time available (BTA) plans offer an attractive option. Rates are lower under these plans, since stations cannot guarantee a time spots will be aired. However, most stations make an effort to rotate ROS and BTA as equitably as possible. When commercial loads are light, they frequently schedule these spots during premium times. Of course, when a station is loaded down with spots, especially around holidays and elections, ROS and BTA clients may find themselves buried. The idea behind these plans is that these advertisers receive a more than fair amount of choice times at rates considerably lower than those clients who buy specific dayparts.

TAP

Many stations offer their clients a Total Audience Plan (Package). It is designed to distribute a client's spots among the various dayparts for maximum audience reach, while costing less than an exclusive prime-time schedule. The rate for a TAP spot is arrived at by averaging the cost for spots in several time classifications. For example, AAA = $80, AA = $70, A = $58, B = $31, thus the TAP rate per spot is $59. The advantages to a client are obvious. While the advertiser may be paying a higher than normal rate for B time, she gets a significant discount on the spots scheduled during morning and afternoon drive periods. TAP is very effective because it exposes a client's message to every possible segment of a station's listening audience with a clear measure of cost effectiveness.

Bulk and Annuals

Advertisers who buy a heavy schedule of commercials over the course of a year can receive bulk or annual discounts. Large companies in particular take advantage of volume discounts because savings are significant. Bulk plans, however, can be very cost effective and therefore attractive to smaller businesses. The idea is to divert the retailer's attention away from the annual cost figure to the *pay-per-use* figure. A bulk plan that costs 10 thousand dollars a year, looks better when presented as $833 each monthly billing period. This overcomes sticker shock. When the client is reminded how much more business this few hundred dollars is going to generate, the whole thing seems pretty reasonable indeed.

Flights and Orbits

Announcements are rotated or orbited within time classifications to maximize the number of different listeners reached. If a client buys 3 drivetime spots per week to be aired on a Monday, Wednesday, and Friday, over a 4-week period, their time schedule differs each day. Here is a possible horizontal and vertical rotation setup.

	MON	WEDS	FRI
Week 1	7:18	6:26	9:09
Week 2	8:21	7:35	8:06
Week 3	6:11	9:12	7:47
Week 4	9:20	8:34	6:52

Rather than purchase a consecutive week schedule, advertisers may choose to purchase time in flights, an alternating pattern (on one week and off the next). For instance, a client with a seasonal business or one that is geared toward holiday sales may set up a plan to schedule spots at specific times throughout the year. Thus, an annual flight schedule may look something like this

Feb 13–19	Washington's Birthday Sale.	10 A 60s.
Mar. 14–17	St. Patrick's Day Celebration Sale.	8 ROS 30s.
Apr. 16–21	Easter Parade Days.	20 TAP 30s.
May 7–12	Mother's Day Sale.	6 AAA and 6 AA 30s.
Jun. 1–15	Summer Sale Days.	30 ROS 60s.

Aug. 20–30	Back-to-School Sale.	15 A 60s.
Sep. 24–Oct. 6	Fall Sale Bonanza.	25 ROS 60s.
Nov. 25–Dec. 19	Christmas Sale.	25 AAA 60s and 20 A 30s.

Let's take a look at the wisdom behind a few of the preceding flights. The client purchases 10 spots in A time during the week that precedes Washington's Birthday to reach the home female audience. The A time on this station is 10:00–3:00 P.M., so a schedule of spots here does a good job of targeting women who work at home. The client uses a TAP plan to move Easter inventory. This will get the client's spot in all dayparts to help him reach as many different people as possible at the best unit price. During the back-to-school days of late August, the client once again targets the strongest female daypart on the station, and around Christmas the client purchases his heaviest flight because this is his so-called do-or-die period (the time when business potential reaches its peak). The heavier spot purchase will help assure success during this crucial time. Selling in flights makes a lot of sense to many advertisers because of its calendar relevance.

Features and Packages

An AE can derive a spot schedule from a rate card to market a station to a sponsor. Most stations offer feature buys and packages. As displayed in Figure 8 in Chapter 3, features allow clients to become associated with popular station programs and personalities. Many clients feel this helps give definition to their use of station airtime (a value-added buy because of the glory-by-association factor). Sponsoring a feature is often viewed as more prestigious than a straight rate card buy: "Billious Brothers Landscaping brings you X109s 'Week in Capsule'."

Sponsorships give the audience the impression that the client is responsible for providing them valuable programming, and this is good PR. Clients often purchase package plans, which include a combination of rate card and feature spots (all rates emanate from the card). A client could end up with a weekly schedule that looks something like this

6 AAA 60s
3 AA 60s
5 A 30s
2 AAA *Traffic* 60s
3 AA *Stocks* 30s

The logic behind such a plan would be articulated by the salesperson during her presentation. Of course, this schedule would have been carefully thought-out before the salesperson approached the client. The *why* of the buy should be perfectly clear to everyone.

On and Off the Rate Card

Rate cards exist to show the dollar value of station inventory (airtime). In a very real sense, radio stations are retailers. Like the corner shoe store whose shelves are loaded with a variety of footwear product (each priced to reflect their market value), the station's stock in trade are increments of commercial airtime; that is what is on its shelves. Therefore, stations attempt to hold fast to stated (published) prices for airtime since most cards are designed with discounting benefits.

If this were an ideal world, everything would go as planned, and no prospective clients would say "Sure, that's what your card says, but what can I really get spots for?" Truth be known, deals *off* the card are made, although the majority of stations do (or attempt to) adhere to the mathematics published in their rate cards. Without a doubt, the objective is to stay *on* card, because working off the card sells that station short or devalues it. The increasing popularity of the grid structure stems in part from the desire to avoid rigidity without compromising the integrity of the rate card. Instead of working under-the-table, an AE can (with approval by station management) step down a grid in a situation that warrants such an act.

The danger in giving off-card deals to clients is that expectations for future breaks grow. Furthermore, word gets out that a particular station's rate card is meaningless, because off-card deals are routinely made. This makes getting on-card rates difficult, if not impossible.

A salesperson should stick to the card. Besides, working below the published rates ultimately affects the salesperson's pocketbook. Clearly, 15% of a $10 rate is better than 15% of a $7 rate. Don't give away the candy store. You may find that in doing so you are also giving away your (and the station's) respect. No one is inwardly impressed with a station that sells under its stated value. It may take some stronger selling to get the on-card rate, but the rewards go beyond dollars and cents.

In conclusion, rate cards can be simple or elaborate. In the end, they are a tool to assist the sales rep in formulating a buy. It should be reiterated that it is often considered a poor idea to leave a rate card with a client to figure out, even when such a request is made. First, few laypersons are adept at reading rate cards, and secondly, (and probably most important from the station's perspective) a station does not like to publicize its rates to the competition, which is what happens when too many rate cards are in circulation. It is quite easy for any station to obtain a competitor's sales portfolio, but stations prefer to keep a low profile as a means of retaining a competitive edge, and in today's marketplace, anything you can do you do. Of course, not all stations feel that rate cards should be guarded. In fact, plenty of stations would probably jump at the opportunity to air drop a ton of their current rate cards on all of the retailers in their listening area.

With all of the preceding in mind, at least hold this one thought—a rate card is a salesperson's ticket to prosperity.

5

The Sales Day

A salesperson who does not use time effectively is a salesperson who is wasting time. Recall the quote at the beginning of Chapter 1—"Time is money." Thus, planning and organizing the sales day are crucial to the successful time-seller.

PLANNING AND ORGANIZING

Plan each sales day in advance. Attempting to plan the events of a day on the actual day is pushing it too close. Make your appointments in advance. Even cold calls must be thought out in advance. It is unproductive to wait until the last minute; opportunities are forfeited. Relying on serendipity is foolhardy. Jay Williams, president, Broadcasting Unlimited offers this observation:

> "Luck is when opportunity meets a plan. Are you prepared—*each day, every week*? Do you know today (Friday) where you'll be going to get business next week? You should! A planned week is crucial to success. And the best time to plan the following week is Friday night—when everything is still fresh. Review your planned week the first thing Monday morning. Your sales will improve dramatically. Do brainstorming and paperwork before 9:30 A.M. and after 4:00 P.M. Yes, you'll be busy for awhile, but tomorrow only comes once a year, so you have to make the best of it. Let me repeat, plan each day, every week. Organization helps you achieve more—helps you get results both professionally and personally. It decreases frustration too."

So then, how to organize the sales day? To start with, your calls are likely to fall into three categories: set appointments, servicing, and cold. In the first instance, since appointments are prearranged, you know when and where you will be meeting with the client. Those calls are already on your call sheet. For example

9:45	Alkay Flooring (callback)
11:00	Eyeland Optical (presentation)
12:30	Marlo's Stereo (lunch meeting)
4:15	Carlton's Corner (presentation)

The salesperson with the preceding appointments may then work out her day based on the location of each call in relation to other prospects. "Be sure to plan your day and week geographically. For example, don't try to be in Westville and Eastville on the same day. Driving time is down time," says Williams.

Assuming the salesperson with the above schedule has taken geography into consideration when making these appointments, she may then construct her day in a time-efficient way. Using the U.S. map as a microcosm of a local sales area, a schedule that has the salesperson driving from New York at 9:45 to Santa Fe at 10:20 and to Chicago at 11:10 is an inefficient one because the salesperson barely has enough time to get from one appointment to another, and even if she does manage this, the morning has consisted of only three calls. There is no time for calls between each of these appointments. When clients are vast distances apart, work your day so that you start with one client in the morning and reach the other one by the end of the day. In between, hit other prospects. Either make appointments to pitch new clients or service existing ones, or plan a series of first calls along the way to your final destination. This is one way to approach the geography imposed by clients set apart by time and space. Obviously, it would be wasteful to take the cross-country call approach hypothesized earlier in this paragraph.

Another point on this theme—every salesperson should become familiar with the land mass (*lay of the land*) within the station's signal. Study road and street maps and directories. Learn the most direct route between two points. A station AE should become as adept at moving about a city or town as a cab driver. Jay Williams said it best, "Driving time is down time."

Make every call (first, second, or third) count. This requires thought. Always have something to show the client. It is not enough to formulate a schedule of calls, you need to develop a plan for each call. There is never a good excuse for not having a clear idea of what to offer (to sell) a client. Establish this while formulating the day's schedule. Make each call and each day count.

Making Appointments

Arranging an appointment with a client does several things, it generates an agreement by the retailer to listen to what the AE has to say—the proverbial foot in the door. For example, getting a prospect to say "sure, drop by around 11:00 tomorrow," is a move toward the goal post. It represents a gain of serious yardage. The AE is assured of an audience. When the client agrees to meet with that station sales rep, she is allotting time for a sales presentation. The act of agreeing to meet with the AE is a positive sign. At the very least, it signifies that a potential for a sale exists.

An appointment helps give design and meaning to the sales day. A call sheet consisting only of cold calls, without set meetings, can seem rather barren to a sales-person. Ideally speaking, most of an AEs calls should be prearranged, because an appointment is a stronger position to start from than an unannounced visit. Clients don't like surprise sales visits.

The telephone is the instrument that makes appointments. The value of the telephone to the salesperson cannot be over-estimated. It is the world's great time-saver. More can be done on the phone than can ever be done on the road. Of course, the road ultimately is where the direct sales rep belongs. However, the effective use of the phone can tighten and focus the day and conserve on gas simultaneously.

There is a right way and wrong way to use the telephone. A prospective client can be forever lost or won in the first few seconds of a telephone conversation. There are many ways to lose, or at least damage, a prospect via the telephone:

> "Hi there! I'm Billy Bob from Super X109—that great radio station that gives away free pizzas twice a day. I'd like to make an appointment to sell you time."
> *Click*!!

The client is going to hang up. Why? It should be obvious from this very blatant example of telephone terrorism. Turn-off number one: no human interactivity. This example is a monologue—a one-way communication. The salesperson launches directly into a high-powered, one-sided, egocentric ("we're that great radio station") spiel. The next mistake perpetrated by this caller constitutes a direct violation of an age-old maxim, never tell a prospective sponsor you called to *sell* him something. Think about it. When was the last time you responded merrily to a caller who used the word *sell*? In fact, when was the last time you heard any caller use this four letter word—"Hi! I'm calling to *sell* you something." *Click*!! This major infraction will get a person's name permanently removed from the membership scroll of the Universal Order of Radio Account Reps.

Do not pitch on the telephone. Do it in person. However, the telephone is the perfect tool to arrange a meeting. This might be a better approach:

> "Hello, Mr. Jennings? Good morning, sir. How are you? This is Billy Paley calling. I'd like to arrange a time to come by and tell you about a very special plan X109 is offering area retailers to increase in-store traffic. This will only take a few minutes of your time. Yes, we are the station that gives away free pizzas twice a day. Good. I'll see you tomorrow at three. Did you say anchovies? Have a nice day."

There are a number of positives in this telephone approach. For instance, there is a degree of interpersonal communication. It is not a monologue as in the former case. The client has participated and has an existence. You have made a human connection. Furthermore, the sales rep exhibits some sensitivity by inquiring about the client. Showing interest on the basic human level conveys warmth and selflessness—two things most of us find hard to resist.

This approach is more effective because the sales rep is merely asking the client to let him drop by with a plan especially designed to increase business. No mention of "selling" something, although this is implicit in the request. You can touch someone just as easily with a feather as you can a hammer, and if the objective is simply to touch someone, why not use a feather. Here the idea is to get in and meet the client face-to-face, so coming on like a steam-roller over the phone is tantamount to using a hammer when a feather will do the job.

Talk To the Decision-Maker

You can use the phone to ascertain who the decision-maker is—who the person is that can say *yes*. If you are unable to connect directly with the boss before heading out on the road, you can usually learn who this person is and when this person is available. This gives you something to go on.

"Hello, is this the manager?"

"No, this is Mary. Ms. Smelling is not in the store until noon each day."

With this tiny, but valuable, bit of information, you know who to approach and when. The telephone is a time-saver. A good salesperson realizes this and gets vital information over the phone before approaching a retailer.

The telephone won't necessarily get you a sale, but it can lead you to one. Don't discourage easily in your pursuit of the appointment. Persevere. Be tenacious without being rude or a nuisance. Always be pleasant on the phone—never pushy or overbearing. However, if you simply can't nail down an appointment over the phone, an in-person call is the next step. For many people, saying no over the phone is infinitely easier than saying no in-person. Unless the prospective buyer has emphatically indicated a total disinterest in talking with you, continue the pursuit. Sometimes it all comes down to timing. So, giving it one more shot may produce the kind of results you've been hoping for. Never underestimate the ability of people to change their mind. I recall giving up on a client who kept putting me off with statements like "Not now" and "I'm just too busy." Weeks went by and on a whim I paid an unannounced visit on this particular retailer, who exclaimed: "How come you never called back? I wanted to talk with you." (Oops!)

Cold Calls

Behind every cold call is the hope for a warm reception. Are cold calls necessary? Yes! Are they worth the effort? Definitely. Some sales people report that a third of their commissions come from cold calls. That should help remove any doubt as to the merit and value of the so-called *off the streeter*.

Perhaps the next question to consider is, Just what is a cold call? or What does a cold call mean? Is a first call a cold call? Well, not always. A first call on a client may be the result of an appointment. However, a cold call is invariably a first call. That is to say, very little (if any) contact has been made prior to the approach—ergo, the word cold.

This should not give the impression that a sales person approaches a strange retailer without any preparation. We're talking cold call, not stupid call. Many cold calls are spontaneous. That is, a sales rep runs across an unfamiliar retailer in the course of her travels and attempts to make contact. It has already been stated that many cold calls are the result of unsuccessful attempts to set up appointments. Although, since some contact has been made, it could technically be argued these are not exactly cold calls. (Ah, semantics!) The thing that all cold calls have in common is that they are unannounced.

Here's a scenario: X109 sales rep Bet Soldman spots a woman's clothing store while on the road between clients. It is three in the afternoon, and Bet's next appointment is not until four. It is only a ten minute ride to her next planned stop, so she has breathing space. Time to make a stop at the store she has just spotted. A sign in the window proclaims "Just Opened!" Bet is surprised that she hasn't heard about the new business, but stores pop up all the time with little fanfare. From past experience, Bet knows brand new retailers are very good prospects, since most are very receptive to promoting their fledgling enterprises. Bet also knows that she should have something to offer the prospect should the situation justify an on-the-spot pitch. Her sales manager has always said, be prepared to make an offer every time you enter a business, regardless of whether it is the first call or tenth call. The ultimate aim of any sales call is to make a sale. This doesn't mean Bet will press for a sale. Her primary goal is to introduce herself—to make a first impression and gather a first impression, which hopefully will lead to an order. Bet collects her thoughts before entering the store. She knows what plan to present if the atmosphere is conducive, but essentially she is prepared to say hello and set up an appointment for a presentation. In the course of her conversation with the prospect Bet is determined to learn all she can to aid her effort to sign the client.

Stations expect, nay require, direct-retail AEs to make cold calls. A lot of new business is generated that way. The actual percentage of sales stemming from cold call call-backs is very impressive indeed, and this is how salespeople help build a clientele (a list, something discussed in Chapter 6).

In order to succeed, especially on the small direct-retail level, a station sales rep has to warm up to cold calls. After awhile, a salesperson develops considerable cold call savvy—the more you do it, the better and easier it gets. Many salespeople develop the attitude that the cold call is really a welcome wagon sort of function, and that helps ameliorate any anxiety that is created by venturing into the unknown.

"Good afternoon. I'm Bet Soldman from X109, and I just stopped by to congratulate you on your opening. The store looks wonderful. We can be of help in letting everyone know you're here..."

"And so it goes," to cop a phrase from novelist Kurt Vonnegut, whose books often probe the meaning and value of that four letter word—time.

How Many Calls?

There is a saying: "you have to make the calls to make the sales." This is a pretty good saying. But how many calls are enough? This really depends on the level of sales to a great extent. A salesperson who primarily works agencies may actually make fewer calls than the salesperson involved in direct-retail sales, because agency appointments on average run longer. An AE may spend an hour at an ad shop but twenty minutes with a retail account. Of course, this varies. In some instances the opposite may be true.

In terms of how many actual calls a direct sales rep should make, the conventional wisdom from the sales manager side is that a well planned day makes possible 2-to-3 calls an hour. "If a sales person gets out and makes this many calls a day, every day, this person is going to make a good income. Quantity and quality make a good team. Make a lot of calls, and make good presentations, and you're going to succeed," observes WBZs director of retail sales, Glen Lucas.

The law or rule of average is at work here. The more calls a salesperson makes, the better her chances of making a sale. Some sage advice from another expert: "Get out! Don't sit around the office sipping coffee. The best time for sales, according to the RAB, is from 10:00 A.M. to noon and from 4:00 P.M. and 5:00 P.M.. Yet too many people are in the building during those hours doing paperwork. This should be done before 9:00 A.M. and after 5:00 P.M.," contends Jay Williams.

PERSONAL GOALS AND STATION QUOTAS

When I was new to the profession, my sales manager asked me, "How much do you want to make?" He continued, "You can make as much as you want. It is up to you. You're in the driver's seat, son. That's what's so great about radio sales. Only you set the limits on your income." No station is going to say, "Hey, wait a second, fella'. You're bringing in to many accounts and making too much money. If you don't cut back we'll have to get rid of you." Not a likely occurrence.

Since a salesperson is ultimately responsible for how much he can earn, it is important to establish personal goals. Never mind what the station sets as your so-called nut to crack (a weekly or monthly billing goal). Regard this as a minimum objective. For example, if the station sets your monthly billing quota at 15 thousand, shoot for 20. Never be satisfied with what other people establish as your goal—set your own. Satisfy the management, but once again, no station is going to express displeasure with an AE who exceeds quotas.

Of course, a salesperson must have a carefully devised plan for reaching his personal income goal. It takes energy, effort, and drive to reach a goal, but few professions offer as much chance to determine one's financial fate as does radio sales. In the last chapter of this book, some of the nation's top sales executives talk about what it takes to succeed.

SALES MEETINGS

Station sales managers hold meetings for a number of reasons, among them to disseminate information, direct departmental efforts, and motivate sales people. For the inexperienced sales rep, they serve to educate. For example, during a routine sales meeting the following subjects may be discussed: presentation approaches, recent list changes, quotas, personal experiences with clients, new rate card and package options, and collection strategies.

One of the special functions of many sales meetings is to serve as a brainstorming opportunity. Jay Williams notes

"A sales meeting allows you to tap into the collective tank, so to speak. Use each other as resources. Break the isolation. Don't work alone. You have a lot of talent among you. Each morning you can discuss who you are going to sell, the ideas you will use—why the client will buy your idea. In a sales meeting you can help each other with ideas. If you have problems, they can be discussed in the morning confab. A sales meeting should constitute an opportunity to brainstorm and share feelings and concepts about the market."

Sales meetings motivate the sales force. "Do the Vince Lombardi thing," as my sales manager often put it. Clearly, it is important to get the sales staff in a positive frame of mind before letting it loose on the world. A salesperson who greets the day without enthusiasm is not going to survive. Sales meetings can serve to pump up and focus the rep. Of course, no salesperson should rely on external stimuli. The zeal has to come from within, but it doesn't hurt to get some outside encouragement.

6

▼
▼
▼ **Prospecting and List**
▼ **Building**
▼

Among sales circles you invariably hear the comments "She's got a killer list" or "I'd die for his list." These remarks stem from understandable envy, because a killer list is the equivalent of a fat bank book. However, each sales rep has an opportunity to create a profitable roster of clients (see Figure 13).

THE LIST

Each salesperson has his or her own list of customers, and from the standpoint of most reps these lists are sacrosanct (other sales reps in the station must keep their hands off). To paraphrase a popular bumpersticker—"You toucha' my list, I breaka' you face." This list may reflect geographical territories and be skewed toward particular types of accounts such as car dealerships, clothiers, and restaurants. More often than not, it is more random in its design.

When a radio station hires a salesperson, she is customarily provided with a list of accounts to which airtime may be sold. For an inexperienced salesperson, this list may consist of essentially inactive or dormant accounts, that is, businesses that either have been on the air in the past or those that have never purchased airtime on the station. The station expects the new sales rep to breathe life into the list by selling spot schedules to those accounts listed and add to the list by bringing in new business. This is called list building, and it is the primary challenge facing the new account executive.

It is challenging. Trekking down memory lane once again, I recall my own initiation into the world of account lists. On the heels of my very first sales meeting, I was invited into the sales manager's office and presented my list. "My," I thought, "what a lot of businesses, and they're all mine. Good lord, I'll be rich in no time at all." I was handed a list 2 pages long, single-spaced. It contained the names of 75 area retailers. Noting my all too apparent glee, the sales manager informed me "They're not all active. In fact, I think only a couple are on the air right now." When my glee shifted to disappointment, he quickly added "But there's some real good prospects on there. A lot of them have been on before, so they know we do a good job. I'm sure with a little encouragement you can get them back on."

It was apparent after 73 calls, even to this wet-behind-the-ears sales rep, that the list was not about to make anyone rich. Sure, there were some maybes, possibles, and could-bes that needed to be groomed, or regroomed, but the majority of the

Local Radio Advertisers Include
A Wide Range of Businesses

Share of Expenditures

Rank	Total	1M+	250K-1M	50K-250K	Under 50K
			Market Population:		
1. Auto Dealers	10.7%	11.1%	11.2%	10.9%	10.2%
2. Dept. Stores	8.4	9.4	8.6	7.9	8.1
3. Banks	8.0	6.5	6.6	8.3	9.1
4. Clothing Stores	7.7	7.2	7.4	7.6	8.1
5. Restaurants	7.0	6.4	7.7	7.2	6.8
6. Supermarkets	6.7	6.4	6.0	5.3	8.1
7. Furniture Stores	6.4	4.7	6.6	6.2	7.3
8. Bottlers	5.9	6.0	6.5	6.9	4.9
9. Appliance Stores	4.9	3.5	5.2	5.0	5.2
10. Savings & Loans	4.2	5.0	3.6	4.4	3.9
11. Shopping Centers	3.3	4.2	3.6	3.8	2.4
12. Jewelers	3.3	3.2	3.1	3.6	3.3
13. Theaters	3.3	6.7	4.1	3.1	1.4
14. Lumber Dealers	2.8	1.0	1.9	3.0	4.0
15. TBA Stores	2.8	2.9	3.3	2.6	2.6
16. Drug Stores	2.5	2.2	1.6	2.3	3.4
17. Shoe Stores	2.0	1.2	1.8	2.1	2.3
18. Entertainment	1.7	2.6	2.5	1.8	0.7
19. Agricultural	1.3	0.1	0.7	1.6	1.9
20. Stereo/Record Stores	1.2	2.8	2.0	1.0	0.2
21. Other Financial	1.2	1.5	1.0	1.1	1.1
22. Religion	0.6	0.2	1.3	0.7	0.3
23. Real Estate	0.5	0.8	0.2	0.6	0.5
24. All Others	3.6	4.4	3.5	3.0	4.2
	100.0%	100.0%	100.0%	100.0%	100.0%

▶ *Figure 13*   *Local radio advertisers include a wide range of businesses. Courtesy RAB.*

accounts on the list (I referred to as the *Dead Sea* scroll) went beyond dormant to moribund. They had been neglected for too long or horribly mishandled when they were on the station. The prognosis for their return was bleak but not altogether hopeless. Time and tremendous effort might inspire some action. I clung to such a hope. Time brought the realization that this so-called account list was just a place from which to start; a syllabus for a how-to course in reality management.

In retrospect, the list provided valuable encounters with a wide assortment of retailers, and although it bore little monetary fruit, the experience was priceless. I learned that every salesperson must build his own account list, almost always from scratch, regardless of the number of active advertisers a list contains. With this hard won wisdom, I set about the task of infusing my list with new client blood, and in a matter of weeks I had constructed an animated account roster. In the immortal words of Dr. Frankenstein, (a world-class builder of things that breathe from things that don't) "It's alive!!"

Active lists that generate commissions, are traditionally given to more experienced radio salespeople. A salesperson may be persuaded to leave one station in favor of another based upon the contents of a list that include large accounts and prominent advertising agencies. Lists held by a station's top biller invariably contain the most enthusiastic radio users. Sales reps cultivate their lists like a farmer does his fields. The more the account list yields, the more commissions in the salesperson's pocket.

To reiterate, a list that contains dozens of accounts does not necessarily assure a good income. If those businesses listed are small spenders or inactive, little in the way of commissions will be generated and billing will be low. The objective of list building is not merely to increase the number of accounts, but rather to raise the level of commissions it produces. In other words, a list that contains 30 accounts with 22 of them active, is more preferable than one with 50 accounts containing 12 that are doing business with the station. A reasonable deduction. A salesperson does not get points for having a lot of names on his list.

List Shift

It is the sales manager's prerogative to shift (reassign) an account from one salesperson's list to another's if she believes the account is being neglected or ineffectively handled. At the same time, in-house accounts handled by the sales manager, may be added to a sales rep's list as a reward for performing well. A sales manager may pare down a salesperson's account list if it is disproportional with the others at the station. A salesperson may cause a brouhaha if the sales manager trims their account to make an equitable distribution of the wealth. The sales manager attempting this feat may find herself losing a top biller. Thus, she must consider the ramifications of such a move and proceed accordingly. This ultimately may mean letting things remain as they are. The top biller often is responsible for as much as 30–40% of a station's earnings.

List Organization

Some salespeople stratify their lists to more effectively exploit their potential. Here are categories often used by the organization-conscious sales rep:

Actives:	accounts currently on the air.
Strong prospects:	accounts about to sign.
Possibles:	those needing more work, but worth it.
Unlikelies:	all but cold, but another call could warm things.
Inactives:	could be called "forget its," but there is no such category in radio sales.

Organizing a list helps the AE determine how to focus attention. Of course, the idea is to move as many accounts into the *Actives* category as possible. Before writing off any *Unlikelies* or *Inactives*, give it another well planned shot to move the client up the category ladder. The so-called dead-ones have fooled AEs by suddenly and unexpectedly coming to life and climbing a rung or two toward the *Actives* stratum, and more than once a dead-one has ascended directly to this revered level. Never give up hope, and never forget an account.

PROSPECTING

Where do you find a client? This is what prospecting is all about, and it involves a search to yield a paying customer. There are many sources of information salespeople rely on to help ferret out prospects: newspapers, yellow pages, other electronic media, current clients, personal and professional contacts, direct mail flyers, and billboards.

Newspapers

Radio sales reps use newspapers to find area retailer advertisements. Like it or not, it is a fact that newspapers remain the preferred advertising medium for most retailers, especially in smaller markets. So, the local newspaper is a wealth of information for a station sales rep, because it reveals who is out there, who is spending money, how much money is being spent, and what is being promoted. Let's evaluate each of these infobites:

Who Is Out There?   If you forget what retail gems your market contains, newspaper ads serve to remind you. Reviewing newspaper ads is a very good way to keep current and prevent prospective clients from slipping through the cracks. In a small city there are hundreds of businesses, so surveying the print media is a good way to keep track of who is out there;

Who Is Spending Money?   Clearly newspaper advertising costs money, so the fact that a store is promoting itself through the press tells you it has an advertising budget. This is an important qualifier. If a retailer can spend money on print, it can spend it on your station;

How Much Money Is Being Spent?   The size of a retailer's ad reveals how much money they spend, since the larger the ad the more it costs. This is important indeed. It tells you the extent of the retailer's monetary commitment to promotion. The number of ads in a single issue and how frequently the ads appear over a period of time contribute to this awareness;

What Is Being Promoted?   The look and content of the ad is invaluable in helping a radio rep prepare a plan to bring to the newspaper user. The print ad usually attempts to convey data pertaining to the retailer's image—how it wants the public to perceive it—and what it is marketing (its product). From this, an AE can develop copy and investigate possible co-op tie-ins (co-op is discussed in Chapter 13).

Yellow Pages

Telephone yellow pages provide the same prospecting value as newspapers (review the infobites above). This is essentially a local area encyclopedia of businesses that advertise. Every business listed in the yellow pages (with anything other than a regular one-line entry) pays for the privilege. The yellow pages constitutes the most comprehensive directory of local businesses, and, to make life easier, businesses are listed according to what they do or offer. Many sales reps consider the yellow pages the single most important prospecting source.

Electronic Media

Other radio stations and television and cable outlets are good prospecting sources as well. A client's involvement with another station proves he has already been convinced of the value of using the electronic media for advertising purposes. In other words, the account has already been sold on radio, for example. Just because the account is on another station doesn't rule out its being on yours. What the sales rep must do is compose an argument for the account to spend money on another station as well. This means an additional buy for the client or a complete switch over to your station. The rationale for this action must be made amply clear in the plan, that may include audience data proving unequivocally that X109 reaches the listener the retailer is after (and reaches more of them), spot and feature rates attractively competitive with the station the client is currently on, and copy possessing a more creative presentation of the client's marketing message.

In any event, sales reps monitor other stations to determine what businesses are advertising and how they are advertising. It is common practice for stations to assign AE's stations to monitor, because it is valuable to know what the competition is doing.

Client Referrals

Establishing a strong relationship with a client can lead to other rewards. Once you have gained the respect of a sponsor, because you have delivered on your promises, he may be helpful in leading you to prospects. No retailer operates in a vacuum. Retailers often belong to local business associations, and their contacts can become yours. Don't hesitate to ask a client if he knows other retailers who may benefit from an ad campaign on your station.

Personal Contacts

As a member of a community, a sales rep develops friendships with a variety of people, including those who have retail businesses, work for retailers, or have friends who do. Any successful salesperson will tell you the value of networking. This doesn't mean that every person a sales rep knows should be exploited as a means for reaching someone who may buy an advertising schedule. But maintaining an alertness for connections that may prove of value and exploring those possibilities when appropriate is not sociopathic behavior, unless it manifests in this form:

> "Say, Bill, we've been friends for quite awhile, eh?" observes John, an X109 sales rep.
>
> "Three weeks," reflects Bill.
>
> "That long, huh? Listen, here's a piece of paper. How about listing every relative and friend who you think might buy time on my station? Isn't your wife's father the owner of Pascales Dry Cleaning? Better give me his home phone number. Didn't you mention that your mother has a little business on the side? She must have a few bucks to spend..."

Obviously, John has a thing or two to learn about human relations. There is a time and place for everything, not to mention manner. Granted, the above is an over-dramatization, but relationships are routinely harmed by insensitivity and aggressiveness (you can attract more bees with honey than you can with vinegar). No friendship should be put in jeopardy for the sake of getting more business. On the other hand, friends are usually willing to help out real friends.

Billboards and Flyers

Every day a sales rep passes advertising billboards and (if she is like everyone else) receives direct mail advertising. As a society we are inundated by advertising messages that come to us in a variety of formats. The highway billboard is among the most ubiquitous. Billboards are seldom an inexpensive proposition, and there are a number of problems inherent in this type of advertising, which will be discussed later. Any retail outlet that uses billboards is a prospect for station airtime. This holds true as well for stores that use direct mail flyers. The simple fact is, any retail business that is already engaged in marketing itself to the public is a prospective radio user.

PROSPECTING DATA

Information accumulated during the prospecting process is valuable and should be filed in a sensible way for future reference. Build a file for each prospect. The more an AE knows about a would-be client the better the plan he can develop and prepare. A clipping file is easy to maintain. Cut out newspaper ads and place them in files, along with copies of yellow page display ads, direct mail flyers, station monitoring reports, and so on. Don't rely on memory, because too much happens in the course of an average sales day. Gathering and maintaining data is fundamental to the job of time-selling.

DECLARING PROSPECTS

This harkens back to the idea of sales rep account lists. The strategy behind prospecting is to build a list. Of course, every sales rep in the station is busy at this too. This invariably leads to complications when two sales folks attempt to list the same client.

Unfortunately (or fortunately depending on your perspective), many stations often are reluctant to post or distribute account lists among AEs. This is regarded as tantamount to divulging income levels.

"You have those accounts!? Geez, you must be making a killing!"

Jealousy, envy, resentment . . . demands! So AEs are left to establish an account's availability before pitching. Redundant sales calls are an inevitable side-effect of this age-old system.

Thus, once a sales rep has located a potential client it is a practice to *declare* that business to the sales manager, who then must determine whether that particular account is free to assign. Most stations operate on a first-come first-served basis. This means the sales rep who declares the account first usually gets the account.

When the account is already on another rep's list, this generally puts the issue to rest. However, the sales manager may decide to remove the account from the list it occupies and reassign it to a sales rep who shows greater potential of doing something with it. When two reps declare an account simultaneously, say in a sales meeting, the sales manager decides which rep will get the listing.

RECORD MANAGEMENT

We touched upon this, but it is a subject that deserves a little more attention. A sales rep may have over a 100 active and inactive accounts, and each of these represents a gradient on the earning potential scale.

Keep a record of all client calls, whether they occur over the phone or in-person. It is easy to forget what transpired with a client you had contact with two days ago, not to mention a month ago. A record of the call will put you back on point. When preparing a record of a call, the more detail the better.

> Bennington Floor Covering—contacted 5/11. Presented TAP Plan. Client says not interested until late July. Wasn't too impressed with TAP approach. Listens to "Bill Bannon Show." Maybe have Bannon visit on next call. Offer plan in show. Call back in mid-July. Gets co-op dollars and buys in combo. Not happy with newspaper. Likes station. Solid prospect. Mail new inserts from media kit and drop off dozen X109 magnets. Stick with this one.

Is better than this

> Bennington Floor Covering—Contacted 5/11. No go 'til July. Call back then.

The former provides abundant data on which to reacclimate to the account for the next call, whereas the latter gives the AE nothing to go on.

A current status report, like the one above, should be kept in every client's file for quick and easy reference. The account file should also include information on past plans offered to the client, as well as complete information on the plan currently in use—this includes a copy of the signed contract outlining the buy. The file should include copies of all past contracts as well as affidavits and credit check data. Credit checks are traditionally conducted to determine a new client's viability—solvency. If the bill doesn't get paid, the sales rep doesn't get his commission.

A client's file should contain all information germane to the buy. Good records are invaluable to a sales rep. Be as innovative as you like when maintaining client records. Just make sure your method doesn't undermine your intent.

7

The Market and the Client

In order to help a retailer plan an effective on-air advertising campaign, a sales rep must be thoroughly familiar with the market in which both the station and client operate.

MARKET DEMOGRAPHY

A station sales rep must be able to answer several general market questions

What is the age breakdown of the population?
What is the gender breakdown of the population?
What is the ethnic profile of the population?
What is the socioeconomic makeup of the population?
What is the area's primary industry?
What is the general state of the area's economy?
What is the economic outlook for the community?

Very basic information indeed, but vital to any sales rep planning a campaign for a prospective advertiser. Many sales reps know about their station but precious little about the market served by their station. A new salesperson, particularly if new to the area, should exert a genuine effort of acquire some market savvy. It quickly becomes evident to a retailer when a station rep has little knowledge of the area, and this creates a negative impression because the client cannot help but wonder "How competent is this person?" This is an understandable reaction. Here you have a sales rep telling a prospect that he is there to help enhance the retailer's status in the community, and the rep hasn't the vaguest idea of what constitutes the *community*. This is the equivalent of someone claiming to know how to fix a car when he has never looked under the hood.

There are numerous ways a salesperson can become knowledgeable about the market. Nearly every station conducts a market study. This means that the station has data that can inform and enlighten. Most stations include market/audience data sheets in their media kits. For starters, a sales rep should assimilate this easily accessible information. This may be the tip of the iceberg. Inquire as to the existence of other market research. In this day and age even the smallest stations find it crucial to learn as much as they can about the town or city in which they are doing business.

If the station lacks market data, there are other sources outside of the station. The Chamber of Commerce usually is an excellent source of information on local business-oriented topics. City hall may also possess an archive containing useful data. When all else fails, there's always the public library, and rather than attempt to locate material on your own (assuming a lack of familiarity with the library) talk with the reference librarian. Tell this person your objective.

Local residents can help you get a sense of the community (in terms of what influences have had the most significant impact on the area and citizenry). Talk with people (neighbors, friends, colleagues) and become as familiar as possible with their perspectives regarding the place in which they reside. Don't rely soley on published statistics. Do some reading between the lines and numbers.

ASSESSING THE COMPETITION

A salesperson has to know what she's up against in terms of the other advertising media that are out there attempting to woo retailers. As the saying goes *know thine enemy*. Of course, *enemy* is too strong a word to describe other media sales reps, especially our good radio brethren.

Other Radio

Despite what some old and hardened sales folk might say, it is not really a war out there. Although sometimes it can seem like a battle. Here's the scene: you're a sales rep for X109 in a market with six other radio stations, two of which air a similar format. Your station is a low-power AM in a predominantly FM market, and we know the plight of AMs. To complicate things, those two other stations pursuing a like demographic are high-power FMs. Is this the ultimate nightmare? No! Every station has something unique to offer, and that includes X109. It is the sales reps responsibility to know that and to be amply aware of his own station's virtues.

Get to know everything possible you can about the proverbial *other guy*. You'll find vulnerabilities, but moreover this will help you discern your own station's strengths. Obtain the other stations' media kits and analyze the material. You can orient your own client plan by being an expert in what the competition is offering.

Talk to retailers about their experience with other radio stations. Don't do so in a deceitful manner, but convey sincerity. In other words, you want to know completely about the client's advertising history in order to put together a *viable* proposal. That should be the impression you give during your questioning. Never be afraid to ask pertinent questions, but do so with tact and decorum.

Another very valuable way to gain knowledge of the competition is to monitor other stations. Tune in the other guys. Find out what they're all about—what they're selling out on the street. Develop a critical checklist on each station. Something along this order

- What is their target audience?
- How well do they execute their programming?
- What are their chief strengths?
- What are their chief weaknesses?
- How effective is their signal?
- What is the quality of their spot production?
- What is their spot load?
- Who are their heaviest users?

It is not the goal of becoming familiar with other radio stations to bad mouth them, but rather to better understand the other players in the game so that you may better play your *own* game.

Some radio sales philosophers resist classifying other stations as competing media in an attempt to create a sense of fraternity among sales reps. While this is a noble concept, other stations do compete for the same ad dollar. Of course, fratricide is a heinous crime, and that is how the competition views *switch-pitching*.

Newspapers

In an attempt to placate those idealists, let us discuss other competing media because radio stations are hardly the only ones courting retailers. Newspapers constitute radio's most formidable competition. This has been the case from the beginning and is not likely to change any time soon. It is therefore imperative that radio AEs gain familiarity with local print media. Small rural markets often have one newspaper, but usually small markets adjacent to urban areas have several. Newspapers have become the trusted advertising medium for most retailers. Why? Well old habits are hard to break. Many retailers have a long history of involvement with newspapers and have regarded radio buys as supplemental for almost as long. Whose fault is that? The sales reps who have worked these accounts. Radio is not a secondary advertising medium, yet too many retailers perceive it as such.

Newspapers as an advertising medium are not without their deficits. Over the past few years gross circulation has dropped, advertising costs are high, and their demographics are older—typically over thirty. (Chapter 9 discusses overcoming client objections.) For now, it's sufficient to say newspapers are not a panacea, but they do have a considerable hold on the purse strings of many retailers. So, a sales rep who becomes familiar with the print media gains insight into the prospective clients attitude about this considerable adversary.

Television

Television is not as significant a competitive threat as might be imagined, especially on the small market retail selling level. This is true because most retailers find TV cost-prohibitive. No one would question the effectiveness of television advertising. The consumer habits of the world are a testimony to TVs efficacy as an advertising entity. However, only a few small retailers can afford to promote their businesses over the picture tube. Direct-retail radio sales reps in smallish markets are seldom put in the position of competing with the video medium for advertising monies. When this occurs, however, there are a host of drawbacks to television use that may be enumerated for the benefit of the client's ears. (These are discussed in Chapter 9.) Although television does not represent a great opponent in the quest for small retailer ad budgets, it should not be dismissed. TV sales reps are out there, and they do pick fruit in these orchards. Therefore, it is a wise radio sales rep who analyzes local TV outlets as she does other radio stations. The checklist (as outlined above) for assessing the audio medium can be applied to the video medium as well.

Cable

During the past decade cable literally exploded on the scene. Today over 11 thousand systems are in operation nationwide, and many of these originate programming geared for a specific audience demographic; this specialized programming is offered to local businesses for sponsorship. Sound like a familiar strategy? Programming employs sales reps who peddle time, announcers, programmers, production people, and so forth, and the size of their staffs are often comparable to area radio stations. Another thing that town cable systems and radio stations share in common is the fact that costs for advertising time is inexpensive, as compared with broadcast television and newspapers. This makes cable a very real competitor. At least one that must be factored into the competition equation. Some cable channels work in league with local radio stations to offer retailers a *combo* or mixed media advertising opportunity. However, this is more the exception than the rule.

Only recently have radio station sales departments fixed a wary eye on the machinations of area cable systems. The direct-retail sales rep should join in this scrutiny, because for many local businesses the idea of being on the television set is a very alluring one, and it is made all the more alluring by the often reasonable advertising rates the coaxial medium offers.

So, once again the advice is to tune in and assess the relationship of the cable company with the local advertising community. Determine the extent (if any) of the cable system's involvement in the grand and glorious quest for sponsors. Learn who invests ad dollars in the system. Yes, get possession of their media kit and rate card. Inquire as to their effectiveness for clients, and above all ascertain the system's reach. How many households subscribe to their service, and what is the nature of this service—how many channels do subscribers receive. There are inherent weaknesses in cable advertising (see Chapter 9). Think of this, your station may be one of three in the area, but when a client buys time on the local cable system her ad is going out on one of perhaps 50 available channels and to *only* those households wired for cable. Keep in mind too that the local cable channel represents fertile prospecting ground, so watch with a pad and pencil close at hand.

Billboards, Posters, and Flyers

Billboards and posters (mostly of the mass transit variety) cover the landscape in most areas, even the most pastoral settings are not immune to outside advertising. Motorists and pedestrians are usually the target of this type of advertising, and it certainly can be very effective, given that some billboards and posters are striking in their use of the visual medium. The drawback from the retailers perspective is that this is one of the most expensive forms of promotion. Billboards have a number of other shortcomings. For one, they are only noted by 36% of their intended audience, according to Outdoor Advertising Incorporated. Outdoor advertising poses the least competition to the direct-retail sales rep, but they should not be dismissed. If for no other reason, a salesperson should take inventory of the area businesses that employ this medium. Occasionally an advertiser tailor-made for what radio has to offer (and what advertiser is not?) is convinced by a persuasive outdoor ad rep to invest in *signs*. This constitutes a good lead.

Local businesses are fond of direct mail promotion because it can be very customer-targeted. That is to say, a mailing can be directed to a specific demographic and geographic grid. However, since this form of advertising is not inexpensive and because the world in general has developed an abhorrence of what is unaffectionately referred to as *junk mail*, the appeal of this approach has lost some of its glamor over the last few years. However, in certain markets direct-mail advertising is more than alive and well, and therefore must be dealt with. Sales reps can learn a lot by perusing the messages of these insidious missiles which pour through the mail shoot with alarming regularity and volume.

"My God, the author is actually suggesting we read that stuff!" Yes! Reading can be profitable . . . if not fun.

THE CLIENT

The client is the most important person in the world and should be treated accordingly. A pretty strong statement indeed. But it's this attitude that makes sales. Forget yourself and think of the client—be *client-oriented.* "Learn everything you can about a prospective client. Know their needs as well as they know them. Set out to help them, not to sell them," advises Jay Williams. No doubt about it, the more a sales rep knows about a client the better the results for everyone involved.

The Client's Market

Up until now, we've discussed general market characteristics and competition from the radio station's perspective. Now it is time to assess these from the client's. What is the client confronted with? For example, using the client *shoe store* model, it is important to ascertain who is the shoe store's perceived competition. Once this is ascertained, other questions necessarily follow:

How many other shoe stores are there?
Where are they located?
What is their size?
What do the stores look like?
What products do they carry?
How is their product priced?
What product(s) do they emphasize?
How long have they been in business?
How much do they advertise?
On what media do they advertise?

There are more than a few retailers attempting to sell a product that is not in-sync with area pocketbooks, interests, and sometimes even geography. I recall a client who was convinced that his Alpine ski shop would do a brisk business once word got out. We tried our best to make his hopes materialize, but alas, it became all too obvious that downhill ski equipment and apparel was not high on the list of planned purchases by those living in St. Petersburg, Florida. It was not so much the idea that people don't buy snow skis in the Sunshine State, because many Floridians head north in the winter to enjoy the sport, so having an outlet of this sort made some sense. The real problem was the fact that the city in which the business was attempting to operate had a predominantly senior-citizen population and was a major retirement community. This was just not a real good retail venture. The station did what it could, but in the end realized the dilemma and to its considerable credit, attempted to make this conclusion known to the sponsor.

The question in such situations: What is the role of the sales rep? First and foremost she must gain an understanding of the client's intended customer and then evaluate the prospects for attracting this customer. The investigation should show that you are dealing with a viable enterprise. If not, try to help anyway. You never know. It wouldn't accomplish much, other than to embarrass or alienate a client, to inform him that his store doesn't stand a sandwich's chance at a fat farm of surviving. Discretion is the better part of valor. Besides, brilliance and ingenuity in an ad campaign have been known to perform miracles. When all is said and done, know what you are getting into, and bring your full powers to the occasion.

Following a careful and thoughtful investigation of the prospect's intended market, an evaluation of the retailer's inventory, physical plant, staff, and location are necessary. Concerning inventory

What does the client sell?
What is the price range of goods?
Does the product reflect current market trends?
How well stocked is the store?

Regarding the physical plant (the appearance of the store) these are some considerations:

Is the store visually attractive?
Are goods displayed in a sensible and appealing way?
Is there ample parking?

The next point to ponder has to do with the staff. Sales clerks can make or break a retail outlet. Look for answers to these questions:

Are there sufficient sales people to serve customers?
Are the sales people courteous and friendly?
Are they knowledgeable about the store's product?

Yet, another point to evaluate is location:

Where is the store located in relation to other things.
Is it easily accessible?
Is it in a high-traffic area?
Is it suitably identified?

These are all questions that deserve answers. There are more questions for each of these points, but these should serve to give you an impression of what is involved in educating yourself about the client. Remember, you can't adequately aid the retailer without an appreciation of his environment.

In the end, an in-person interview with the would-be client concerning his perspective, vis-à-vis the business, customer, and market, can be very illuminating.

Determine the client's business approach and philosophy concerning all things terrestrial and otherwise. Beyond dollars and cents, what does the client want to get personally and professionally out of the endeavor? What is the client's ultimate goal? It is rarely just to make money. Anyone who goes into business will tell you that a piece of their soul goes into it as well. It's good to become more intimate, to become an empathetic *human* being. People reveal more when they feel they can let their guard down. There's nothing wrong with showing you can be a friend as well as a professional radio sales rep.

Often one of the more interesting conversations with the client concerns his portrayal of his customer. Your author recalls the following conversation with a prospect:

"What kind of customer are you looking to attract, Mr. Wisassnow?"
"Rich ones!"
"Right, but what type of customer do you hope to bring into your store?"
"Ones with lotsa' bucks."
"I understand, but why do you think your store attracts the customers it does?"
"They need what I got."
"Why don't they shop elsewhere?"
"They like my good looks and charm, and I sell good stuff cheaper than the other guys."

Finally, information that revealed something. Mr. Wisassnow's last comment conveyed at least two things worth contemplating. To him the secret in bringing customers to his store was friendly, attractive service (that personal touch) and competitive prices. From Mr. Wisassnow's point-of-view, these were central reasons why his business drew paying customers. A further discussion with this retailer provided more insights, which helped focus the advertising plan, thus making it all the more pertinent.

The objective of the chapter, has been to impress the sales rep with the need to look beyond the station's closet of goodies to the world outside—the world where the retailer functions. You've heard the expression, "you've got to put yourself in the other guy's shoes." This is especially true when selling time.

INDUSTRY NOTES BY JAY WILLIAMS

The first call, gathering information.

1. The setting: First observe, is the office neat and organized or messy? Is the person hurried, methodical, energetic, sour? What style of person are you dealing with? Success depends on going to the client on his or her own level. If the setting is full of interruptions (telephone calls, people coming in and out), say to the client "This meeting could ultimately help you a great deal in developing your advertising and marketing strategy, and it would only take a few minutes if we could be uninterrupted. Would you mind if I closed the door (if you held your calls, etc.)?" You must control the environment for the meeting.

2. Opening or rapport question (suggested): First, you may want to comment on something positive you see in the store or in his office. It's an ice-breaker. Of course, try not to do anything that puts the client off (never smoke during a sales call). It sends the wrong message. Always take notes when talking with the client. It lets the client know that what he says is important to you. Always lean forward or sit attentively. Do not sit on a sofa when a chair is available. It makes you look unbusinesslike and too relaxed. Sales calls must have intensity to be effective. Now the question: "It seems like an interesting (busy, exciting . . .) business; what did you do before and how did you get here managing/owning this store?" This, or something like this, gives the client the opportunity to talk about himself and his real motivations for being in the business, and that will ultimately tell you how to sell him.

3. Transition: "In order to talk to you about advertising and marketing your business, I'd just like to ask you a few questions so I know more about your business and what you're trying to accomplish. The more you can tell me about what you feel is important, the better we will be able to help you. First, what makes your store really unique? Why do customers come here rather than to your competition?"

4. "Who do you consider to be your major competition? Why?"

5. "If you were going to give me a customer profile, what kind of people come and buy in your store—age, sex, and income?" Then ask "Do different types of people buy different types of products (services), or do pretty much the same type of people buy all the products in your store?" (Try to get into product and market segmentation and see if they're different.)

6. "I'm sure some of the products (services) you sell are more important than others, especially from a profit or growth stand point. What are the most important products (services) in your store from a profit perspective?" Then follow up with, "In looking at your business, particularly in the future, which products do you see dramatically increasing (adding to your growth) and which products or services do you see declining?" And follow up with, "Do you see any new products or innovations that will effect your business?"

7. "Do you have an advertising theme (or positioning statement) that reflects your business?" Believe it or not many will not. If not, then ask, "If you can, please try to describe your business to a customer or potential customer in one sentence." This request usually provokes thought and that's good.

8. Mechanical questions: "Do you or your products or services have co-op available, and do you use it? What are your best times of the year for business? Do you do most of your business during the end of the week and

weekends, or is it different from that? Is there anything unusual about your flow of business that I should know about?"

9. "We've talked about the growth and the direction of your business a little bit, but we haven't talked about your short term goals. What problems, especially consumer-oriented problems, are you trying to solve now?" It may be a product or service, it may be a time of day that's weak, it may be a particular season. Probe to find out what he's trying to solve in the near term.

10. "Long term, what do you see are the greatest obstacles or problems that need to be solved in terms of growth or increasing your business?" Probe here also.

11. Advertising and marketing: "In looking at your advertising and promotions in the past, which have been the ones that you remember as outstanding—that really worked for you?" Then follow up with this: "Which ones were a real disappointment? Why?" You need to know the reasons why he felt these things worked or didn't.

12. Results: "What kind of results did you get with these successful promotions?" You need to get him to quantify or qualify what success means to him. Did he have thousands of people? Did he sell lots of merchandise? Did he create a lot of awareness? What was success?

13. "Is there anything about your business or your competitor's business that gives them a major advantage over you—or vice versa? In other words, is there a major strength of your business that your competitor doesn't have?"

14. "Is there anything I have not asked that you think is important for me to know about your business or your advertising over the past year?" This will let you know if he thinks there might be something coming up, and it will get you and he thinking more long term.

15. Follow up: "I'd like to take this information back to both our creative and marketing people—we generally have a weekly meeting as well as several smaller sessions—and go through this information. Then I'd like to come back with some ideas and suggestions for you. Could we get together at this same time next week?" Making the next appointment right there is crucial.

16. Noteworthy: Send a follow up note to the prospect. One or two lines is more effective than a whole letter. You don't have anything to say at this point anyway. Just thank the retailer for his time and information, and reconfirm your appointment.

8

The Presentation

Few sales are made on the first call. Nonetheless, the salesperson does go in with the hopes of *closing* an account.

> "You say you want to sign on? Gee, sorry, but this is my first call. I'm just here to gather information. Maybe next time."

Sure! A good salesperson gets the order whenever the opportunity presents itself. Although the first call generally is designed to introduce the station to the prospective sponsor and determine its needs, the sales rep should always be prepared to propose a buy that is suitable for an account. This means that some homework must be done relative to the business before the approach is made—even if it is a first approach. "Never walk into a business without some kind of offer in mind, should the prospect indicate a desire to get the ball into play right away," suggests WBZ's Glen Lucas.

"Always be prepared to execute the 'Four Ps' of the sales presentation:

1. *Problem* Establish the need. Ascertain what is preventing the retailer from enjoying more business.

2. *Plan* Demonstrate how your station can address this need and improve the retailer's business. 'Taking advantage of our highly focussed midday features will attract the demographics you're after.'

3. *Package* Explain the spot buy that will be effective. Detail its inherent value.

4. *Pitch* Make the close! Get the order! 'So let's put X109 to work for you. Give me your okay and we'll get started.' "

If the initial call goes smoothly, the salesperson may opt to go for an order immediately. If the account obliges, fine. In the event that the prospective sponsor is not prepared to make an immediate decision, you should make a follow-up appointment. Make a call-back as close to the initial contact as possible to prevent the impression from fading and growing cold. The primary objective of the return call (if a presentation was made during the first call) is to close the deal and get the order. To strengthen the odds, the salesperson must review and assess any objections or reservations that may have surfaced during the first call and devise a plan to overcome them. Meanwhile, the initial proposal may be beefed up to appear even more attractive to the client, and a *spec tape* (see Chapter 12) can be prepared as further enticement.

Ten Tips For Sales Presentations

Customers are changing. "Power closing" techniques are rapidly becoming the ways of yesteryear. Your customer today is:

• Experienced as a buyer just from living in this generation.

• Expecting more than ever from you - everyone claims to be best.

• Informed better about everything, thanks to information access.

• Skeptical - when was the last time you saw anyone press hard with their pen when signing a contract?

Make your sales presentations come to life and sell more. Commit to these 10 principles of effective sales communication and watch the results roll in.

1. Be sincere - speak heart to heart with your clients. People make decisions with their emotions. Logic is used to justify or overturn the emotional decision. Even if you think the media buyer has no heart, they still operate with their gut instincts.

2. Prepare for every sales presentation by focusing on the client's expectations. No one cares what you want to talk about. They only care about what they want to hear.

3. Speak about objections on the customer's mind. If both of you avoid the unpleasantness of discussing these things, you can never overcome them.

4. Personalize your message. Talk to your customers with rock-solid eye contact. If you don't look at them, they don't have to look at you.

5. Be enthusiastic. Be positive and upbeat about what you are selling. Attitudes are contagious - make sure yours are worth catching.

6. Body language contributes the most to the impact of your message.

7. Seeing is believing. Find ways to visualize your presentation with simple charts, graphs, pictures or appropriate visual aids.

8. Rehearse your presentation out loud.

9. Edit yourself unmercifully. Commit to maximum impact in minimum time.

10. Inspire customer confidence with yours. Most importantly, if you work to understand the customer's interests and devise a way to satisfy them, the first half of the sale is made. You will have sold yourself on the merits of your proposal. This enables your confidence to soar, with sales results right behind.

Frank Carillo is Sr. VP of the Executive Communications Group, a New York-based management communications consulting firm with clients in North America and Europe. He may be reached by Pulse readers at 212/513-1221.

▶ *Figure 14   Ten tips used to succeed in sales presentations. Reprinted with permission from* The Pulse of Radio.

Should the salesperson's efforts fail the 2nd time out she makes a 3rd and even 4th (15th, 16th . . .) call. Perseverance does pay off, and many salespeople admit that just when they figured a situation was hopeless an account said that magic word, "yes." "Of course, beating your head against the wall accomplishes nothing (unless your goal is to bruise yourself). You have to know when your time is being wasted. Never give up entirely on an account. Just approach it more sensibly. A phone call or a drop in every so often keeps you in their thoughts," observes radio sales expert Ron Piro. (See Figure 14.)

DO'S AND DON'TS

Two checklists follow. The *do* list contains some suggestions conducive to a positive sales experience, while the *don't* list contains things that will have a negative or counterproductive effect.

Do

- Research advertiser. Be prepared. Know all you can. Have a relevant plan in mind.
- Be enthusiastic. Think positive.
- Display confidence. Believe in self and product. You have something *good*.
- Smile. Exude friendliness, warmth, and sincerity. Be human and accessible.
- Listen. Be polite, sympathetic, and interested.
- Tell of the station's successes. Provide testimonial material.
- Think creatively. Look for the novel approach.
- Know your competition.
- Maintain integrity and poise.
- Look your best. Check your appearance.
- Be objective and retain proper perspective.
- Pitch the decision-maker.
- Be courteous to everyone you encounter.
- Ask for the order that will do the job.
- Service the account after the sale.

Don't

- Pitch without a plan.
- Criticize or demean client's previous advertising efforts.
- Argue with the client. This just creates greater resistance.
- Talk cost up front.
- Bad-mouth competition.
- Talk too much.
- Brag or be overly aggressive. Avoid the *me* word.
- Lie, exaggerate, or make unrealistic promises.
- Smoke or chew gum in front of the client.
- Procrastinate or put things off.
- Be intimidated or kept waiting an unreasonable amount of time.
- Make a presentation unless you have client's undivided attention.
- Use jargon unknown to client.
- Lose your temper.
- Ask for too little. Never undersell a client.
- Oversell a client. Don't pitch after client is sold.
- Fail to follow up.
- Accept *no* as final.

Checklists like this one are always incomplete and can only serve as basic guidelines. Anyone who has spent time on the street as a station account person can expand on this or any other checklist. For the positive-thinking sales rep, every call gives something back, whether a sale is made or not.

OBJECTIVE OF THE BUY

A single spot on a radio station seldom brings instant riches to an advertiser. However, a thoughtfully devised plan based upon a formula of frequency and consistency will achieve results. Radio sales manager John Gregory contends, "It has to be made clear from the start what a client hopes to accomplish by advertising on your station. Then a schedule that realistically corresponds with the client's goals must be put together. This means selling the advertiser a sufficient number of commercials spread over a specific period to time. An occasional spot here and there doesn't do a whole lot in this medium. There's a right way to sell radio, and that isn't it."

Our list of *do's* and *don'ts* of selling suggested that the salesperson "ask for the order that will do the job." It also said not to undersell an account. Implicit in the first is the idea that the salesperson has determined what kind of schedule the advertiser should buy to get the results expected. Too often salespeople fail to ask for what they need for fear the client will balk:

"Did you say 450 a week? !*#+$%! Are you kidding? I want you to leave my store right now, and don't you every come back! 450?! I'm calling the police, fella'."

Fear of such imagined outbursts have inspired the coward in us all, but in the end an ineffective plan will offend the client much more. Don't settle for what you can get without much resistance. This, in fact, may be doing the advertiser a disservice, since the buy that you settle for may come up far short of declared objectives.

"It takes a little courage to persist until you get what you think will do the job. There is a temptation just to take what the client hands you and run, but that technique usually backfires when the client doesn't get what he expects. 'You told me $25 a week in spots on your station would increase store traffic by 20%.' As a radio sales rep you should know how best to sell the medium. Don't sell it short. Don't be apologetic or easily compromised. Sell the medium the way is should be sold. Write enough of an order to get the job done," (Ron Piro).

Inflated claims and unrealistic promises should never be a part of a sales presentation. Avoid

"If you buy spots on my station you'll have to hire additional sales people to handle the huge crowds. Is there enough parking to handle, say, four thousand cars? You better get plenty of rest before your commercials start running, because they're never going to let you alone."

Salespeople must be honest in their projections and in what a client may expect from the spot schedule purchased: "You'll notice a gradual but steady increase in store traffic over the next few weeks as X109's audience is exposed to your commercial." This is the better approach. Unfulfilled promises tend to come back to haunt you, ruining any chances of future buys. Too often salespeople caught-up in the enthusiasm of the pitch make claims that cannot be achieved. Radio is a phenomenally effective advertising medium. This is a proven fact. Those who have successfully used the medium can attest to the importance of placing an adequate order. "An advertiser has to buy a decent schedule to get strong results," notes Piro. A radio sales axiom says it best: "The more spots aired the more impressions made, and the more impressions made the more impressed the client."

OUTWARD AND INWARD APPEARANCE

On our *do* list it is suggested that a salesperson look her best before a client. The first impression is usually the one that sticks. Surface impressions generally are what reach us first. They reveal much about a person before she opens her mouth. Nobody wants to engage in a business relationship with someone slovenly dressed, because this conveys weakness of character, which in the end usually means failure.

In the 1980s a popular book on the subject really said it all in its title, *Dress For Success*. While appearance alone does not guarantee success, it certainly is an important factor. How you look is a reflection on how you perceive yourself and your world, and how you look reflects your station as well.

There is no prescribed uniform for sales reps nor should there be. But common sense should dictate that extremes in attire are to be avoided. In other words, no retro-hippie, tie-dyed, bell-bottomed hip-huggers for a call on the local hardware store, or anywhere else for that matter. Concomitantly, a tuxedo and black tie would be inappropriate as well. Overdressing raises questions in the client's mind: "Wow, check out this guy's rags. This station must cost an arm and a leg. He's making some big bucks." Sure, you're not about to wear Gucci from head to foot in your call to Discount World. But the point here is to convey respectability and stability. Don't generate resistance simply because you want to make a fashion statement. A good rule of thumb is no extremes. Stay away from the wardrobe department of Universal Studios. Generally speaking, go more conservative than avant garde. Why construct obstacles with your apparel? On the other hand, be yourself. No one is suggesting that you buy your clothes off-the-rack at the U.S. Department of Labor either.

What is inside you is a part of your appearance. People develop the perception or idea of you from two levels, so despite the old saying "You are what you wear," the inward self plays a major role. In different words, clothing cannot conceal the fool for the fool invariably surfaces. Selling is a very human experience, therefore the qualities of the sales rep's personality make or break the day. Here are some universal *turn-offs*: insincerity, aggressiveness, arrogance, hostility, aloofness, and egocentricity. Here are some universal *turn-ons*: sincerity, humor, compassion, intelligence, and sensitivity. To get to the heart of the matter, make sure the turn-ons appear and the turn-offs disappear. Adjust your internal tie. If you fail on the personal appearance level, you are doomed to fail on all others. Remember, every call is a personal appearance.

INDUSTRY NOTES BY ALAN CIMBERG

Stop selling and start helping. The really successful salesperson doesn't sell at all. *Sell* is a vulgar, four-letter word. Get out of your mind the idea that you must sell someone and replace it with another four-letter word: *help*.

The difference is that sell is something you do to someone. Help is what you do for them. Selling is an attitude and prospects can sense when salespeople don't have their best interests at heart.

The old-school salespeople are thinking: "You have my money in your pocket, and I'm going to get it." That's the way they come across to prospects. Naturally, the prospect draws away both physically and mentally. We have to stop selling and start helping. The primary objective in selling is to help. It's an attitude, a conditioned way of thinking. It's a positive power that is always present in the professional salesperson. Nothing happens until a salesperson helps somebody buy something. Helping means zeroing in on the client's need and then fulfilling it. That helping spirit separates the mediocre, pavement-pounding person who wonders why he or she can't see results.

Ask questions. Time and time again, salespeople will moan, "The prospect didn't know what he wanted." The real problem is usually that the salesperson does not know what the prospect wants. The way to find out is to ask intelligent questions to qualify the sale. This helps you avoid overloading the clients with choices and isolates what is most important to them.

Ask your clients where, when, what, who, how, and why. Put *why* last because, unlike the other question words, why gets you an opinion. Once you know what your clients want, you can help them get where they need to go.

Your doctor asks you quite a few questions before he hands you a prescription. Talk to your clients, and ask them questions. People love to be sought. They welcome understanding and caring questions about themselves and their needs.

Customers need to know you care. The opposite of love is not hate, it's indifference. People don't mind waiting, but they mind being ignored. All it takes is a look in the client's direction and a warm smile that says, "I'm giving you my undivided attention."

Talk benefits, not just features. Any convincing sales presentation answers the prospect's question, "What's in it for *me*?" Talk benefits. People buy things not for what they are, but for what they will do for them. The important words to emphasize are *you* and *your*. When prospects tell us that something costs too much, it means we have not given them enough appropriate benefits or reasons to buy.

The old medicine show hawker really had benefit-selling down pat. He used a great attention grabber, created excitement, then ran off the list of benefits: "This great elixir cures lumbago, arthritis, and baldness." Finally, he'd ask for the order: "Step right up and pay only 50 cents for the huge economy size." He had the selling basics, including a positive attitude, but he lacked the most important ingredient for long-term success, truth.

Close the sales without stress. Many salespeople fail to ask for the order through fear of being rejected, disappointed, or humiliated. This attitude becomes a self-fulfilling prophecy. Take a positive attitude on closing. You're helping customers make a decision that will bring them desired benefits. Watch for subtle buying signals, like "Sounds pretty good," or "That would be very helpful."

Remind yourself of these items before each sales call:

- Customers buy when they are enthused about your product, price, and company. They won't be if you're not.
- What objectives do you see yourself achieving?
- What problems can you solve for them?
- What benefits will you offer?
- What are your answers to the most often raised questions?
- Since you will never fail to ask for the order, what specific order will you recommend?

When salespeople switch their emphasis from selling to helping the prospect, they move into the true professional ranks.

(The preceding is reprinted with permission from *The Pulse of Radio*.)

9

▼
▼
▼ **Overcoming Objections and**
▼ **Obstacles**
▼

Objections are a part of life. Do you know anyone who has lived life without encountering an objection? The true measure of a salesperson is how he deals with objections.

DEALING WITH *NO*

Overcoming common objections is a necessary step toward achieving the sale. Here are some typical *put-offs* presented to radio sales reps.

1. Nobody listens to radio commercials.
2. Newspaper ads are more effective.
3. Radio costs too much.
4. Nobody listens to your station.
5. We tried radio once, and it didn't work.
6. We don't need anymore business.
7. We've already allocated our advertising budget.
8. We can get another station for less.
9. Business is off, and we haven't got the money.
10. I'll have to discuss it with my associates.
11. We need pictures to sell our product.

There are countless rebuttals for each of these statements, and a knowledgeable and skilled radio salesperson can turn such objections into positives. Let's take a look at some possible responses (RSPS).

Nobody Listens to Radio Commercials
RSPS: if that were true there would be no commercial radio industry at all. Today there are nearly ten thousand commercial stations in operation, tuned by the majority of Americans several hours each day. Prestigious and well-managed businesses use radio because it has been proven extremely effective. Companies like General Motors and Pepsi are not known to invest in things they know don't work. The radio commercial is one of the most powerful forms of advertising ever devised. That's what makes radio a multi-billion dollar industry. Radio works, and it can work for you.

Newspaper Ads Are More Effective

RSPS: Nobody would argue that newspaper advertising is ineffective. However, radio has the ability to better target your specific clientele, whereas newspaper demos are skewed to the over 30-year-olds. Keep in mind that radio gives you audience exclusivity when your message is aired, whereas with newspapers your ad is one of many on the page, unless of course you buy a full page ad, and that is very expensive. Many advertisers use radio in conjunction with newspapers to more effectively reach their customers. One other thought to consider is the fact that most newspapers have experienced a decline in circulation while their ad rates have actually increased.

Radio Costs Too Much

RSPS: As compared to what? It is less expensive by far compared to the major newspapers, television, and billboards. In fact, statistically speaking radio is the most cost-effective advertising medium. It is cheaper to reach one thousand persons on X109 than with any other advertising source in town. Keep in mind that radio is the most user targeted medium, so a dollar invested with us is a dollar that is going to find your customer.

Nobody Listens to Your Station

RSPS: If nobody listened to our station, we would not be in business, much less be making a profit. Many of your fellow retailers regularly utilize X109 to get their messages out to the public. For example, here is a letter from ACE Floor Covering expressing their satisfaction with us. A recent survey conducted by Halper and Associates revealed that X109 is number one in 24- to 32-year-old females; the exact group you say you're after. By your own admission, you want a medium that reaches your customer. Well, that seems to be us.

We Tried Radio Once, and It Didn't Work

RSPS: Sorry to hear that. I'm sure you were disappointed, but I have to ask you not to reject one of the most effective advertising mediums on earth because your one experience was unproductive. Like anything else, radio must be exploited for all of its potential. In other words, sometimes plans are simply insufficient. This may have to do with any number of things: the time of day spots are aired, the number of spots aired, the sound of the spots, or it may simply have to do with the audience reached by the station, which may not be consistent with that sought by the advertiser. I'm not even going to ask you what station you were on. Obviously it wasn't the right one for your particular needs. What is more important is to show you how X109 can meet the goals you wish to reach.

We Don't Need Anymore Business

RSPS: You mean you're already making all the money you want to make? That's today, but radio advertising is an investment in the future, a guarantee that you'll continue to enjoy success. With the ever shifting population, staying visible (and radio gives you *visibility*) is the best way to stay viable. People forget very quickly. Radio advertising is a great reminder that your store is the best place to go. I'm sure you want your business to continue to thrive, and we do too.

We've Already Allocated Our Advertising Budget

RSPS: Very well, but let's consider the next budget period. X109 has a plan that goes into effect around the time of your new budget, and we'd very much like to be a part of your future advertising efforts. The next 6 weeks will give us time to coordinate our efforts and energy to guarantee a successful collaboration. What I'd like to do is reserve a participation slot for you in this unique and special offer, which is likely to go quite rapidly.

We Can Get Another for Less

RSPS: There's always something cheaper out there, but is it better or even as good? Our rates are very competitive, but when compared with some stations we are higher. There's a reason for that, which is important for you as a radio advertiser to know. As I've mentioned, X109 draws more young females than any other station, and you are out to reach the young female consumer, right? So while we get a couple of dollars more per commercial, we deliver 50% more audience in this demographic. If you analyze these figures, we're ultimately cheaper and more cost effective than the other stations. You get more audience and for less.

Business Is Off, and We Haven't Got the Money

RSPS: What you're saying is your business is sick and you're not willing to give it any medicine. When business is slow that's when you need to advertise the most. Rather than accept the situation, do something to change it. Consider this: what if business never gets better? How long can you hang on? Don't become a self-fulfilling prophesy statistic. Battles are seldom easily won, but the first step toward victory is action. X109 can certainly help stimulate and reinvigorate your business.

I'll Have to Discuss It with My Associates

RSPS: You indicated that you made the advertising decisions. Am I correct? And you also expressed a desire to get this plan into action. You admit it is a good plan, so who would disagree? Besides, when all is said and done, the buck stops at your desk, right? Time is wasting. The station inventory might slip away. If you feel the need to get the okay from your associate, why not give her a call right now, so that I can reserve the availabilities before another sponsor takes them. We both know this is right for you, so let's get the ball rolling.

We Need Pictures to Sell Our Product

RSPS: Radio is the theater of the mind. Your commercial will create pictures no television station can produce without costing you a fortune. In fact, the plan X109 has offered you is especially designed to increase the volume of sales in this particular product area. Believe me, in no time Rainbow Vinyl Toilet Seats, Inc. will be on everyone's mind. With a slogan like: "There's a pot of gold at the end of every Rainbow—Vinyl Toilet Seat" you can't miss. (See Figure 15 for suggestions on how to counter cable television advertising.)

There are countless responses for every objection cited and not cited here. Knowing your product and market, knowing the client's product and market, and being able to think on your feet will keep objections from defeating you. Always be

Anti-Cable Selling Strategies

Irwin Pollack, president of Boston-based In-Station Sales Training, offers these key points:

1. Most people subsribe to cable for the pay channels (HBO, Showtime, Disney, etc.) — channels which have no advertising.

2. According to the Cabletelevision Advertising Bureau, children aged 2-11 account for the dominant share of viewing in cable households. Retailers want shoppers, not shoplifters!

3. In a 1988 Roper study, 85 percent of cable viewers reported there were some cable channels they hardly ever watch.

4. The cable audience is not regularly measured.

5. "Homes passed" is a measurement of cable viewership often confused with reach. It refers only to the number of homes where cable is available, not the number of actual subscribers.

6. People watch cable programs, not cable stations. This is important if your local system sells ROS or packages of different services.

7. Cable reaches just over 50 percent of all homes nationwide. Radio has passed 98 percent.

8. When you buy cable what do they give you? A remote control to change channels — often during commercials!

▶ *Figure 15   In recent years cable has become a formidable competitor in certain markets, although the bottom line still looks stronger for radio—as evidenced by these strategies. Reprinted with permission from* The Pulse of Radio.

prepared for objections and stalls. They are a part of the selling experience. Except them as such, and be equipped to transcend them. Remember, on the other side of every objection lies a sale. Some final words of wisdom on this topic by Jay Williams, "Deal with objections directly and swiftly, then go back to the main theme of your pitch. Stand up for your rights. Don't be intimidated. Believe in your product, and hold your head up. Overcome the objection and move on to the sale." Figure 16 lists several reasons why radio gives its clients a competitive edge.

PERSONALIZING REJECTION

Many sales people become demoralized when a prospect rejects a proposal. This reaction is particularly counter-productive. To take a client's rejection personally is totally self-defeating and ultimately debilitating. Remind yourself that you're

COLUMBIA, MO

RADIO ADVANTAGES

The Advantages of Radio

Radio is first in people reach: Radio is the biggest medium, in terms of consumers reached. Radio reaches more different people in a day or a week than TV or newspapers.

Radio is first with primary customers: Key advertising target (adults 18-49, upscale working women, professional/managerial males) spend more daily time with radio than they do with TV.

Radio is first on weekend: Almost 9 out of 10 consumers are reached by radio in a weekend.

Radio is first in the daytime: Radio has always been a leader in morning and afternoon "drivetimes". New research now puts radio as the number one daytime medium between 10 AM and 3 PM.

Radio is first as a news source: Radio delivers the news first in the morning and is the primary news source all day long.

Radio is first with the auto audience: Car radio is so powerful it's almost a total medium by itself. It reaches 7 out of 10 adults in a week.

Radio is first indoors and out: Some 99% of homes have radios. There are almost six working radio sets per home, and battery sets give radio total coverage, inside and out.

Radio is first in speed, flexibility: Advertising can be generated rapidly, without the production and deadline delays of other media.

Radio is first in cost efficiency: Radio's cost-per-thousand has actually risen least of all major media.

Reprinted from a National Retail Merchants Association planning guide for advertising.

P.O. BOX 1345 ▲ 1101 EAST WALNUT ▲ COLUMBIA, MO 65205
314-874-3000 ▲ FAX 314-443-1460

CONTEMPORARY BROADCASTING, INC.

▶ *Figure 16* Radio offers advertisers numerous advantages. Courtesy KFMZ.

a professional dealing with other professionals. You're not asking someone for a date to the prom. Keep your personal feelings out of it, and they won't get bruised.

A problem many sales reps face is getting *up* for the next call after a presentation that has failed. It is easy to become sullen and negative after hopes have been dashed, but remember that last call was just one prospect in a virtual sea of prospects. After a call that doesn't *happen*, rather than wasting valuable time brooding about it, conduct an attitude-erosion survey. "Hunker down and pump up," to quote my former sales manager, who would also say "When the going gets tough, *get going!*" Don't sit around sulking, afraid to go to your next call. Wallowing in self-pity and resignation causes you to sink deeper. Statistics bear out the fact that you have to make the calls to reach the *yes*. Being blown asunder by unwilling prospects keeps you from reaching those prospects who want what you have to offer. Radio sales is not for the meek of heart. Some days can be particularly brutal, but keep in mind that old adage—"Good things seldom come easy." You'll succeed if you don't allow yourself to become defeated. French philosopher Jean Paul Sartre wrote "man creates himself." Think about that, and get to that next call.

REASONS TO ADVERTISE

The reasons to advertise far outnumber the reasons not to advertise. The whole idea behind advertising is to generate business. This is not a new concept. Anyone with a pedestrian knowledge of history knows that the ancient Greeks, Romans, and Egyptians were heavy radio users. Why? Because it worked. Pardon the anachronism, but the truth is timeless.

The radio station sales department at WOOD-AM/FM in Grand Rapids, Michigan (one of the world's great radio stations) has composed a list of ten reasons to advertise. Try to fully assimilate these. They will come in very handy when confronted with some of the aforementioned objections.

1. *You Must Advertise to Reach New Customers.* Your market changes constantly. New families in the area mean new customers to reach. People earn more money, that means changes in lifestyles and buying habits. The shopper who wouldn't consider your business a few years ago may be a prime customer now.

2. *You Must Advertise Continuously.* Shoppers don't have the store loyalty they once did. Shoppers have mobility and freedom of choice. You must advertise to keep pace with your competition. The National Retail Merchant's Association states, "Mobility and non-loyalty are rampant." Stores must promote to get former customers to return, and to seek new ones.

3. *You Must Advertise to Remain with Shoppers through the Buying Process.* Many people postpone buying decisions; they often go from store to store comparing prices, quality, and service. Advertising must reach them steadily through the entire decision-making process. Your name must be fresh in their minds when they decide to buy.

4. *You Must Advertise Because Your Competition Is Advertising.* There are so many consumers in the market ready to buy at any time. You have to advertise to keep regular customers and to counterbalance the advertising of your competition. You must advertise to keep or expand your market share or you will lose to the more aggressive competitors.

5. *You Must Advertise because It Pays Over a Long Period.* Advertising gives you a long-term advantage over competitors who cut back or cancel advertising. A 5-year survey of more than 3,000 companies found
   - Advertisers who maintained or expanded advertising over a 5-year period saw their sales increase an average of 100%.
   - Companies that cut advertising averaged sales increases of 45%.

6. *You Must Advertise to Generate Store Traffic.* Continuous store traffic is the first step toward sales increases and expanding your base of shoppers. The more people who come into your store, the more possibilities you have to make sales. For every 100 items that shoppers plan to buy, they make 30 unanticipated "in-the-store" purchases, an NRMA survey shows.

7. *You Must Advertise to Make More Sales.* Advertising works. Businesses that succeed are usually strong, steady advertisers. Look around. You'll find the most aggressive and consistent advertisers are almost invariably the most successful merchants.

8. *You Must Advertise Because There Is Always Business to Generate.* Your doors are open. Salespeople are on the payroll. Even the slowest days produce sales. As long as you're in business, you've got overhead to meet and new people to reach. Advertising can generate customers now and in the future.

9. *You Must Advertise to Keep a Healthy, Positive Image.* In a competitive market, rumors and bad news travel fast. Advertising corrects misleading gossip, punctures *overstated* bad news. Advertising that is vigorous and positive can bring shoppers into the marketplace, regardless of the economy.

10. *You Must Advertise to Maintain Store Morale.* When advertising and promotion are suddenly cut or cancelled, sales people may become alarmed and demoralized. They may start false rumors in an honest belief that your business is in trouble. Positive advertising boosts morale. It gives your staff strong additional support.

INDUSTRY NOTES BY ALAN CIMBERG

The five words sales people fear most are, "Your price is too high."
You've heard it. You've felt its impact. It stops most of you in its path
just when you thought the sale was going smoothly.

Why is this objection constantly thrown at salespeople? Why do buyers use it so often? The first and most obvious reason is that it may be true. Your price may be too high. More often than not, however, that is not the case. After all, companies stay in business only by remaining competitive.

The primary reasons buyers claim your price is too high is they are looking for a better deal. That's their job. They have to test to see if there is a better price to be had, and they often get it when you cave in. When you hear the words, "Your price it too high," you are being told you have failed in one essential aspect of the sales process: justifying your price. You do that by creating value.

What is taking place in the mind of the buyer is a weighing process. He is evaluating what you have told him or her about features and benefits versus the price you have quoted. If the scale tilts too far in the price direction, the prospect objects. If the scale is balanced, the prospect asks for a better price.

Often salespeople fail to build up the weight of the perceived value of their product. Hence, the weighing process takes place, they lose. It is essential to give your customers all the benefits that are relevant to their needs. This requires extensive product knowledge and the discipline not to trim the presentation through repetition. Too often, sales people get tired of telling the same old story, so they cut more and more pieces out of their presentation. In effect, they short change their prospects themselves. We must remember that the prospect is hearing it for the first time. So make it "first time fresh"—that's what the stage performer does even for the 900th performance.

What does it mean when someone says, "Your price is too high?" There is only one way to find out—ask! Use whatever words are comfortable for you, but tactfully find out the reason for the objection. Then, and only then, can you address the issue intelligently.

There are several possible reasons for being told a price is too high. You might hear someone say, "You're asking $5,000 and I only have $4,500 in my budget." That's one of the easiest objections to handle. Notice that the price is not too high, but the customer just doesn't have the money. Your job now is to work with the customer to find a way to make the sale possible—help the prospect find a way to pay for it, sell the prospect a less expensive package, or show the prospect that his budget is unrealistic for what he needs and maybe he'll find the money.

When asked to elaborate on an objection, another customer may say, "Your price is too high because the competition charges $100 less." This happens most often when the sales person is coerced into giving a price before presenting a complete picture of the relevant benefits. When this happens, it is too easy for the prospect to dismiss your product with an unfair comparison to your competition.

We have all met prospects who were so busy they just wanted to know the bottom-line price. It's easy to cave in and give them what they want, but don't do it. It would be unfair to both of you. A price is meaningless without a value attached to it—and that is the salesperson's job—to attach value. So, be polite, but insist on telling your prospect what she is getting for her money.

Why would a comparison based solely on price be unfair? Most often the comparison is between apples and oranges. So be sure to point out the differences to your prospect. Those differences should be described in terms of features that will be benefits to her for her specific needs.

It is important to have done your homework on your competition before a comparison is made. If you have, you will be able to answer this objection quickly and realistically. Part of a realistic comparison is the discussion of the bottom-line cost that buyers understand so well. Although a competitor's price may be lower, in the long run your station may cost less. For example, you may be able to add value to the sale by throwing in a remote or paying for production.

Remember this: when comparing prices, you have to justify only the difference in price, not your total price. So if you charge $500 and the competition charges $450, you should only address the $50 difference.

Negotiating is a tricky business. It is a custom in some countries to haggle over a price—a process I find uncomfortable. For example, imagine someone offering you a watch that looks pretty good. You ask, "How much?" He says, "$100." You offer him $10 and he says I'll take it.

After the sale, how would you feel? Some people might feel exhilaration because they talked the guy down 90%. Someone else may feel bad because he's wondering how much lower he might have gotten the price if he had tried. In either case, it would make me worry about the quality of the watch. Is it a $100 watch that I got for $10, or a $5 watch I paid too much for?

Negotiations are risky, so always tell your prospect that you have quoted your best price and that you can only be flexible if he can be flexible. Never cut your price unless you get some kind of concession from the buyer. For example, your customer may agree to increase the size of his order or accept a less targeted schedule. You can always remind your customer "You get what you pay for."

Be a pitcher, not a catcher. Don't answer an objection and then pause, waiting for the next one to be hurled at you. That's being a catcher of objections. Instead, move on with your presentation, or better yet, ask for the order!

(Reprinted with permission from *The Pulse of Radio*.)

10

Closing and After

There's a popular song that goes "You gotta' know when to love 'em and know when to leave 'em." This might have been written with the sales presentation in mind. It probably wasn't, but it certainly strikes a familiar note. In this chapter, we'll be discussing the way to make a *graceful exit*. To quote a former sales manager, "If you think getting in was hard, you should try getting out."

THE CLOSE

If you've been observing the ABC rule (Always Be Closing) during your well planned presentation, closing should come naturally. The close depends on good groundwork (preparation). If elements of your plan are vague or lacking in relevance, don't expect to sail out the door with an order in your briefcase.

Again, be client-oriented. Think from the client's perspective. Get into his head, and observe the world through his eyes. What does the client need? How can the plan help the client meet those needs? *What makes sense to the client?* If the plan has been intelligently designed to address the goals of the client, getting to the close should be easy.

Don't get overanxious. Watch for signals during the presentation. As the saying goes: "When you see an opening, *close*." Time is very important. Going for the close prematurely can put the whole thing on ice. Here's a simple schematic: Work your plan—ABC—Address objections—ABC—Get the client to agree with you—ABC—State the cost—ABC—Summarize your plan—ABC—Close.

In the end, ask for the order. Here are some not-so-good closes:

"So, do you want to buy on or what?"
"Ready to sign your life away?"
"Sign in blood right here, okay?"
"Are you interested in signing this contract?"
"Would you like more time to think about buying this?"
"Gimme' your signature on this document."
"Sign here, so we'll have a legally binding agreement."
"Sign here or I'll kill myself."

None of these are probably going to be very effective, except maybe the last one. The point is, don't come across as a beggar or a head-banger. Be neither apologetic or overbearing. The following closes will likely inspire more positive results:

"Give me your okay, and we'll set the plan into action."

"Let me have your approval right here on this line, and I'll put X109 to work
for you."

"This is going to be very effective, and your okay will make it happen."

"Traffic will increase as soon as we get your go-ahead to air the commercials
we just talked about."

"Bet you'll be happy to move that stock; your okay right here will get the customers in here."

There are numerous variations, but integrate the close into your presentation.
Don't isolate the close from the plan. It shouldn't jump out of a dark closet like a
serial killer in a horror movie. Don't scare off a client with something like this

"... so we're particularly effective in reaching the very audience you're
trying to attract to your store. Tell me Mr. Prospect, you'd be happy to
increase your store traffic by 20%, right?"

"Well, sure, I guess. But I don't understand ..."

"Okay! Sign here and make out the check to X109."

Mr. Prospect, feeling pressured and confused, is going to head for the hills, and
this is a shame because he was so near to signing. Stay alert and wait for the right
moment. Asking for a signature in the middle of an objection isn't what you'd call
great timing. This sort of thing just conveys to the client the fact that the sales rep
isn't listening and is only there for himself.

Let the presentation take you to the closing point. A client generally wants the
full story before given the ending. If you tell the story well, the potential sponsor will
be engaged when you reach the closing scene. In fact, if you've done your job well,
the client will want the close.

Just as it is vital not to dash to the closing prematurely, it is imperative to stop
running once you've reached the finish line. In their eagerness, and perhaps insecu-
rity, many sales people lose a sale by overselling a client. When a client reaches the
go ahead point, they don't need to hear any more. When a sales rep fails to recog-
nize the signing stage, a very real danger exists that the opportunity has passed. Put
yourself in this client's shoes.

"And X109 will give you a very special new sponsor discount on
top of the excellent plan I've just mentioned."

"Really? Well, that sounds good."

"And you can be sure that the majority of those morning drivetime spots will air between 7:30 and 8:00."

"Excellent."

"As I mentioned, all the midday spots will be aired in the 'Oldies
Lunch Box Time Machine'."

"Fine."

"Did I tell you about the reach of our signal at night?."

"Yeah ... I think so."

"Let me go over the last part of the plan once again ..."

▶ *Figure 17* *On the front the bumper sticker states the obvious; on the back is a call for a unified order of radio sales reps. Courtesy of Communication Graphics and* The Pulse of Radio.

Sign the guy, for God's sake! At this point, this sales rep is selling the client out of buying on. Some sales reps actually suffer from *closing anxiety*, that often manifests in a form of verbal excess. For some poor souls, the idea a client wants to sign on is too good to be true. These misguided AEs are actually fearful that what they sense is just a fanciful illusion—and why face the horrible reality of a turndown by asking for the order. This poetic refrain by Alfred DeVigny gives some relevant advice about closing a client.

"Silence alone is great; all else is feebleness...
Perform with all your heart your long and heavy task
Then as do I, say naught..."

Good advice. If a centuries dead French poet knew how to close a prospective radio advertiser, there's no reason why you can't learn to do likewise. (See Figure 17.)

RESIGNING

The all-important hyphen has been deliberately left out of the heading in order to make a point. Too many sales folk cop an attitude of resignation once they've signed a client. There are far too many one-time-shots out there in radio direct-retail salesland. Too many sales reps allow themselves to become defeatists, "Why bother going back because the plan probably failed to live up to promises anyway." With this attitude, the rep resists the notion of *re-signing* a client. It's a plain fact that a sales rep cannot expect to live long and prosper on one-time-shots. The idea is to build an account list into something solid and profitable. On the callback it should not only be the intent of the sales rep to re-sign the sponsor, but it should also be his goal to get more dollars from the account—to get a larger share of the sponsor's ad budget. This is possible if the initial plan was good and the sales rep has serviced the account.

There are numerous approaches to re-signing a client. Staying in touch with the client from the start is useful. For one thing, it allows the sales rep to monitor increases in the client's business as the result of his involvement with the station. Armed with proof of the station's positive effect on the client, a sales rep has all the artillery he needs to ask for a renewal and expanded buy.

> "We're really pleased that business has substantially improved since the start of your partnership with X109. We're happy to be a part of your success, and we have a proposal that we're certain will insure continued growth and profit."

On the callback, a sales rep should present a new package, or an *improved* version of the original purchase. The idea is to get the account excited all over again and to impress upon him that you've put plenty of thought into the new (improved) proposal. Again, this shows you're genuinely involved in the effort to strengthen the retailer's hold on his market, because you've been doing a lot of hard thinking and homework. Never walk in with the *same old thing*, unless it is absolutely clear that the sponsor loves the same old thing. Even then, be prepared to offer something else.

Presenting the client with a fresh, new commercial campaign concept is another effective means by which sales reps achieve renewals. Ideally, the new concept should stem from, at least in part, conversations with the client during his initial run on the station.

> "Sal, remember you told me about an idea you had to bring people into your store? I thought it was really good, so I had the X109 production staff put your idea to sound, and you know, I think it's great. Here, give a listen."

Sure, this is a form of client ego-stroking, but so what. If the spots are genuinely good and you're confident they'll do the job for the client without violating the integrity of the station's format, why not go for them? The client cannot help but be pleased that he was an integral part of the creative process designed to make him richer. Remember to think of the client/station relationship as a mutually satisfying and beneficial partnership. Besides, clients know their business better than anyone and often have exceptionally good ideas. Engage the client in every aspect of the plan, and he will feel truly involved and committed (the best possible situation when asking for another order).

A good way to entice renewal is to bring the client some money to defray the cost of the plan—not out-of-pocket money, but co-op dollars. You know what products your account carries, so investigate available co-op funds from manufacturers and distributors. While you'd think your client would be fully aware of subsidies provided by those companies whose products he retails, this is often not the case. If you can locate dollars to assist the client in his advertising efforts, you become a hero, or at least a person with which a sponsor wants to do business. So get out there and do some research. How do you think a client would react to this statement? "And on top of all these excellent values, Mr. Prospect, Ace Tile has indicated they are able to subsidize half of the cost of this plan for you." Manufacturers allocate millions of dollars annually to help underwrite retail efforts to advertise their products. See what is out there. Few retailers are not enthusiastic when a sales rep brings them money. (Chapter 13 discusses co-op subsidy in more detail.)

Retailers are no different than their customers. They love to get something extra for their money.

> "We're also going to make you an official X109 'Star Spot' location. Put this star in your window. When we air a part of the song 'There's No Business Like Show Business,' listeners have ten minutes to get to a 'Star Spot'. The first one who says 'May I have your autograph?' is given a movie pass for two. We air the contest four times each day, so this is a good way to generate some additional traffic. Every morning on the 'Bobby Ray Show,' 'Star Spot' locations are mentioned."

A plan containing incentives, such as this one, is more attractive. We all love to feel we're getting something for nothing. A promotional tie-in is a particularly effective way to *grease the rail*. Sales reps must always be aware of what incentives are available. Never sell incentives only. They are the proverbial frosting on the cake. Sell the cake, then add the frosting.

Bringing new market information to a client is also a good way to induce action.

> "Are you aware that another toilet accessory store is going to open over on Derry Air Road? Of course, with your spots on X109, residents of Citizensville know and respect your business. So I don't think the additional competition poses much of a threat. In fact, with this new plan, they might have second thoughts about opening at all."

Again, knowing the retailer's market is knowing your own. Information that has a potential impact on the sponsor can be used to your advantage—and his. In the end, it is persistently stressing the value of the station that makes the sale, whether it be the 1st or 10th signing situation. Radio sales reps have a truly remarkable product, and this fact should always be made abundantly clear.

SERVICING THE ACCOUNT

"I only see you when you want to sell me something!" Not a good way to be greeted as you enter a client's place of business. It's all uphill from there, and it didn't have to be.

Visit and work with a client on a regular basis. Don't be afraid to appear for fear this will happen

> "Aha!! It's the guy from X109. I've been waiting for you to show up in the flesh so I can cancel my schedule and sue you for false promises."

If a sales rep has constructed a relevant client-oriented plan and has visited the client with reasonable frequency, this sort of thing is not likely to happen. It happens to the rep who signs a client and then vanishes until it's renewal time. A sponsor is going to feel neglected and exploited if you only appear when its time to ask for more money. Don't become a member of the Four F (Find 'em, Flatter 'em, Filch 'em, and Forget 'em) school of selling. There's simply too many salespeople like that. They give the medium a bad reputation, and make it harder for everyone selling radio. Here are just a few reasons to pay regular calls on a sponsor.

To show you're interested and sincerely care.
To make certain the client is satisfied with the commercials.
To ascertain response to the on-air campaign.
To determine if the client would like to increase his schedule.
To leave new station information and promotional material.
To answer any questions the client may have.

Follow-up calls are absolutely vital if a sales rep has any hope of retaining a relationship with a paying customer. Inspect your account list daily, and schedule visits. Don't wait until you get around to it. By then, it's often too late.

On the same hand, don't make a pest of yourself or hang around a sponsor's place of business. This just gives the impression that you have nothing better to do, and how can that possibly be the case since you work at that super, dynamic radio station, X109?

COLLECTING

Few things are as disheartening as an account that goes bad. That is to say, one that fails to pay his bill. Usually the AE collects delinquent sums from past due accounts. He must *right* the account. This is not a favorite thing to do for most AEs, but it must be done because you don't get commission when a sponsor doesn't pay. This fact alone usually provides all the incentive a sales rep needs to go after the overdue billing.

Successfully collecting from overdue accounts sometimes requires considerable virtues, such as perseverance and poise. A sales rep should always give the sponsor the benefit of the doubt, until it becomes apparent that he is not dealing from a position of sincerity. Things do happen, and sometimes a sponsor has a legitimate excuse for not paying a bill on time. Being insensitive or using strong-arm tactics rarely gets the bill paid any faster. Again, put yourself in the retailer's position. Suppose there is a perfectly honest reason why you haven't paid X109, and you are planning to do so as soon as possible. How would you react to this?

"It was just a mix up with the bank and my suppliers, and I'm expecting
a check on Tuesday, and you'll have one on Wednesday."
"I've heard that one before, pal. Think I was born yesterday?"
"Look, I'm telling you that this was just an honest mix up..."
"Do you think X109 cares about that when it's time to pay me my commission check? You're taking food out of my family's mouth. I'll give
you until noon tomorrow or something real bad could happen."

This sales rep learned his technique from the Godfather School of Collecting. It seldom does any good to get nasty, no matter how many times you've tried to collect on your account.

Most stations discontinue air schedules when accounts fail to live up to their obligations. This prevents unpaid balances from skyrocketing. Once a delinquent balance is eliminated, the station may choose to once more avail its services to an account. However, it is likely to insist on payment in advance for future air schedules.

Station billing departments customarily keep a wary eye out for overdue payments, but if a sales rep is wise she'll stay one step ahead of everybody when it comes to this. After all, it is the sales rep who is going to be more directly affected when payment isn't received.

INDUSTRY NOTES BY B. ERIC RHOADS

Here's my resolution for this year and every year. As a member of the radio community, I'll do my part to see the radio industry grow in my community by organizing or participating in an effective market group effort to grow radio. I will focus on positive, logical campaigns that highlight the targeting benefits of our medium. I will not claim radio to be the only medium, nor will I criticize the decisions made by buyers. I will, however, promote radio as a fundamental medium as a part of the overall media mix and point out the areas where other mediums are being improperly utilized.

I will not destroy the creditability of my industry by bashing or bad-mouthing other radio stations. Though I will continue to sell competitively, I will not sell by denigrating others within my industry. I realize doing so hurts the status of all radio.

I will resist the temptation to make a sale when I know it will not fit the needs of my client nor produce results. Though I am under pressure to meet budget, I will not do it at the expense of the client. I understand that short-term thinking may solve today's problem, but may create a bigger problem down the road. I will develop an expertise about my advertiser's business and will become a marketing expert. I will maintain practical-rate integrity and will meet my client's needs by providing active merchandising and promotion campaigns, which I will not give away.

I will focus on developing creative, effective copy that works. I will provide my clients with exceptional service so that when they refer to radio, caring, high quality, and excellent service come to mind.

I will focus on making radio people known as the epitome of professionalism and client focus. I will fight to shed shaky images laid before me by a previous few whose actions tarnished so many. I'm thankful that I'm in radio and will overcome the self-esteem problems of the past. Radio is indeed a first-class medium.

As a manager, I will work to raise the level of stability through my actions. Though I must command positive results and reasonable profitability, I will avoid impulsive decisions resulting in reactionary terminations. I will make it my personal goal to develop an environment and atmosphere that allows employees an opportunity for long-term employment and career growth. I will focus on building the strengths of my people through better communications and continual training. I will encourage their contributions and innovative thinking, and I will listen to what they have to say.

As a member of the radio fraternity, I will uphold the highest integrity and build my radio station within its local community. I will bring new meaning to the words community service, knowing that my contribution will make a difference.

I will be proud knowing that I have been responsible for building radio into the most stable and respected of advertising mediums and have contributed to a positive overall image for radio in my market that has resulted in radio revenues increasing dramatically.

11

Selling With and Without Numbers

"According to the latest book we're number one in over 55-year-old, unmarried, Serbo-Croatian-speaking females, between 2 and 5 A.M. Sundays."

It's great to have the numbers to sell, no doubt about that!

WITH AND WITHOUT

Not all stations can claim to be number one, two, or ten in the ratings. In fact, not all stations appear in any formal ratings survey. Arbitron or Birch do not visit very small markets for the single reason that there may only be one or two stations broadcasting in the area. An outlet in a non-survey area relies on its good reputation in the community to attract advertisers. In small markets, salespeople do no work out of a ratings book, and clients are not concerned with cumes and shares. In the truest sense, an account person must sell the station. Local businesses often account for more than 95% of a small market station's total revenue. Thus, the stronger the ties with the community the better. Broadcasters in rural markets must foster an image of good citizenship in order to make a living.

Civic-mindedness, while always important, is not as marketable a commodity in the larger markets as are ratings points. In the sophisticated, multi-station urban markets, the ratings book is the *Bible*. A station without numbers in this highly competitive environment finds the task of earning an income a difficult one, although there are numerous examples of low-rated and non-rated stations that do very well. However, *no-numbers* puts a metro-area station out of the running for agency business. Agencies almost always buy by the book. A station without numbers works the street, focusing its sales efforts on direct business.

An obvious difference in approach exists between selling a station with ratings and one without. In the first case, a station often centers its entire presentation around its high ratings: "According to Birch, X109 is number one in adults 24–39." Never out of the conversation for very long are the station's numbers, and at ad agencies the station's standing speaks for itself. "We'll buy X109 because the book shows that they have the biggest audience and best point value in the demos we're after."

The station without ratings numbers sells itself on a more personal level, perhaps focusing on its unique features and special blend of music and personalities, and so forth. In an effort to attract advertisers, non-rated outlets often develop programs with a targeted retail market in mind; for example, a home *how-to* show designed to interest hardware and interior decor stores, or a cooking feature aimed at food and appliance stores.

The salesperson working at the station with the cherished *good book* must be especially adept at talking numbers, since they are the subject of the presentation in so many situations. Selling at a top-rated metro station requires more than a casual knowledge of numbers, especially when dealing with agency media buyers. In big cities, retailers have plenty of book savvy too.

Selling without numbers demands its own set of skills. John Gregory observes, "There are really two different types of radio selling—with numbers and without. In the former instance, you'd better know your math, whereas in the latter, you've got to be really effective at molding your station to suit the desires of the individual advertiser. Without numbers to speak for you, you have to do all the selling yourself. Flexibility and ingenuity are the keys to the sale."

To paraphrase a good old song: "God bless the station that's got its own" or "God bless the station that knows what its got."

THE RATERS

The extreme fragmentation of today's listening audience, created by the almost inestimable number of stations and formats, makes the job of research a complex but necessary one. All stations, regardless of size, must put forth an effort to acquaint themselves with the characteristics of the audience. Market researcher Edward J. Noonan says, "A station cannot operate in a vacuum. It has to know who is listening and why." Today, this information is made available through several ratings services and research companies. More stations depend on Arbitron and Birch audience surveys than any other.

Arbitron, the front-runner in providing radio stations with ratings estimates for over two decades, covers over 250 markets ranging in size from large to small. Arbitron claims over 2 1/2 thousand radio clients and a mammoth staff of interviewers who collect listening data from 2 million households across the country. All markets are measured at least once a year during the spring; however, larger markets are measured year round. Until the early 1980s, metro markets traditionally were rated in the spring and fall. However, 6 months between surveys was considered too long in light of the volatile nature of the radio marketplace.

To determine a station's ranking, Arbitron follows a carefully planned procedure. First, the parameters of the area to be surveyed are established. Arbitron measures listening both in the city, referred to as the Metro Survey Area (MSA), and in the surrounding communities or suburbs, classified as Total Survey Area (TSA). Arbitron classifies a station's primary listening locations as its Areas of Dominant Influence (ADI).

Once the areas to be measured have been ascertained, Arbitron selects a sample base composed of individuals to be queried regarding their listening habits. As of this writing, Metromail provides Arbitron with computerized listings of telephone and mailing data, and the company derives its randomly selected sample from the listing. Arbitron conducts its surveys over a 2–4 week period, during which time new samples are selected weekly.

When the sample has been established, a letter is sent to each targeted household. The placement letter informs members of the sample that they have been selected to participate in a radio listening survey and asks their cooperation. Within a couple of days, an Arbitron interviewer calls to describe the purpose of the survey as well as determine how many individuals 12 and over reside in the household. Upon receiving the go-ahead, Arbitron mails its 7-day survey diary, that requires respondees to log their listening habits. A small incentive stipend accompanies the document. The diary is simple, and the information it requests is quite basic: time (day/part) tuned to a station, station identification, whether AM or FM, where listening occurred (car, home, elsewhere). Although the diary asks for information pertaining to age, sex, and residence, the actual identity or name of the participant is not requested. Figure 18 shows an example of a diary log sheet.

Arbitron claims that 65 out of every 100 diaries it receives are usable. Diaries that are inadequately or inaccurately filled out are not used. Upon arriving at Arbitron headquarters, the diaries are examined and rejected if they fail to meet criteria. Any diary received before the conclusion of the survey period is immediately voided, as are those that arrive more than 12 days after the end of the survey period. Diaries with blank or ambiguous entries are also rejected. Those diaries that survive the screening process are then routed through the computer and their information is tabulated. Computer printouts showing audience listening estimates are sent to subscribers. Stations receive the *book* within a few days after the last day of the survey. Arbitron provides subscribers with a multitude of other radio market reports.

Arbitron's most formidable rival in recent years is Birch/Scarborough. As a radio audience measurement service, Birch also provides both quantitative and qualitative data on local listening patterns, audience size, and demographics. Birch interviewers telephone a prebalanced sample of households during the evening hours, 7 days a week, to acquire the information they need. "Respondents aged 12 and older are randomly selected from both listed and non-listed telephone households. These calls are made from highly supervised WATTS facilities," comments Phil Beswick, vice president of Birch/Scarborough broadcast services. The sample sizes vary depending on the size of the market begin surveyed. For example, Birch/Scarborough will contact approximately 11 hundred households in a medium market and between 2–8 thousand in a major metro market.

A wide range of reports are available to clients, including estimates of listening by location (county by county) and other detailed audience information, audience analysis especially designed for small market broadcasters, listening estimates in the nation's smallest radio markets, and so forth.

Dozens of other research companies throughout the country provide broadcasters with a broad range of useful audience information. Many utilize approaches similar to Arbitron and Birch to collect data while others employ different methods. Many stations hire research companies to provide them with data useful in direct-retail sales presentations.

QUALITATIVE VERSUS QUANTITATIVE

Since their inception in the 1930s, ratings services have primarily provided broadcasters with information pertaining to the number of listeners of a certain age

THURSDAY

Time			Station			Place			
	Start	Stop	Call letters or station name. Don't know? Use program name or dial setting.	Check (✔) one		Check (✔) one			
				AM	FM	At Home	In a Car	At Work	Other Place
Early Morning 5 AM to 10 AM									
Midday 10 AM to 3 PM									
Late Afternoon 3 PM to 7 PM									
Night 7 PM to 5 AM (Early Fri.)									

If you didn't hear a radio today, please check here. ☐

▶ *Figure 18* *Log sheet from an Arbitron diary. Courtesy Arbitron.*

and gender tuned to a station at a given time. It was on the basis of this purely quantitative data that most advertisers made a buy.

Since the explosive growth of the electronic media in recent years, audiences have many more options. Radio broadcasters, especially in larger markets, must know more about their intended listeners in order to attract and retain them. Subsequently, there is a need for more detailed information. In the 1990s, in-depth research is available to broadcasters from numerous sources, including Arbitron and Birch/Scarborough.

In this age of highly fragmented audiences, advertisers and agencies have become less comfortable with buying just numbers and look for audience qualities. Audience research expert Christopher Porter notes, "The proliferation of stations has resulted in tremendous audience fragmentation. There are so many specialized formats out there, and many target the same piece of demographic pie. This predicament, if it can be called that, has made amply clear the need for qualitative, as well as quantitative, research. With so many stations doing approximately the same thing, differentiation is of paramount importance."

Today, a station shooting for a top spot in the ratings surveys must be concerned with more than simply the age and sex of its target audience. Competitive programming strategies are built around an understanding and appreciation of lifestyles, values, and behavior of those listeners sought by a station.

HOME-GROWN DATA

Research data provided by the major (and minor) survey houses can be expensive, especially for smaller stations. For this reason, and others, stations frequently conduct their own audience studies. Although stations seldom have the professional wherewithal and expertise of the research companies, they can derive useful information though do-it-yourself, in-house telephone, face-to-face, and mail surveys.

Telephone surveying is the most commonly used method of deriving audience data on the station level. It generally is less costly than the other forms of in-house research, and sample selection is less complicated and not as prone to bias. It also is the most expedient method. There are, however, a few things that must be kept in mind when conducting call-out surveys. To begin with, not everyone has a phone and many numbers are unlisted. People also are wary of phone interviews for fear that the ulterior motive of the caller is to sell something. The public is inundated by phone solicitors (telemarketers), both human and computerized. Finally, extensive interviews are difficult to obtain over the phone. Usually an interviewee will submit to questioning for only 5–10 minutes. Call-out interview seminars and instructional materials are available from a variety of sources, including the telephone company itself.

The face-to-face or personal interview also is a popular research approach at stations, although the cost can be higher than call-out, especially if a station surveys a vast number of individuals in an auditorium setting. The primary advantages of the in-person interview are that questions can be more substantive, visual impressions can be logged, and greater time can be spent with the respondees. Of course, more detailed interviews are time consuming and usually require refined interviewing skills, both of which can be cost factors.

Mail surveys can be useful for a host of reasons. They eliminate the need to hire and train interviewers. This alone can mean a great deal in terms of time and money. Since there are no interviewers involved, one source of potential bias also is eliminated. Perhaps most important is that individuals questioned through the mail are somewhat more inclined toward candor since they enjoy greater anonymity. The major problem with the mail survey approach stems from the low rate of response. Individuals trash 4 out of 5 mailed questionnaires. The length of the questionnaire must be kept relatively short and the questions succinct and direct. Complex questions create resistance, "List all your third cousins, twice removed, who listen to X109" and may result in the survey being violently shredded.

Large and major market outlets usually employ someone to direct research and survey efforts. This person works closely with upper management and department heads, especially the program director and sales manager. These two people require data on which to base programming and marketing decisions. At small outlets, area directors generally are responsible for conducting surveys relevant to their department's needs.

The objective of a survey must be clear from the start, and the methodology used to acquire data should be as uncomplicated as possible. Do-it-yourself surveys are limited in nature, and overly ambitious goals and expectations are seldom realized. However, in-house research can produce valuable information that can give a station a competitive edge.

Sales reps should be familiar with research methods and approaches because the time invariably comes when a client asks the $64 question: "How was this information acquired?" and the response, "Well, I think we bought it from someone" is just not good enough.

RESEARCH SHORTCOMINGS

Although broadcasters refer reverentially to the ratings surveys as the *Book* and *Bible*, the stats they contain are audience-listening *estimates*, no more and no less. Since their inception, research companies have been criticized for the methods they employ in collecting audience listening figures. The most prevalent complaint has had to do with the selection of samples. Critics have charged that they invariably are limited and exclusionary. Questions have persisted as to whether those surveyed are truly representative of an area's total listenership. Can 1% of the radio universe accurately reflect general listening habits? The research companies defend their tactics and have established a strong case for their methodology.

In the 1970s ratings companies were criticized for neglecting minorities in their surveys. In an effort to rectify this deficiency, both Arbitron and Birch instituted special sampling procedures. The incidence of nontelephone households among Blacks and Hispanics tends to be somewhat higher. The survey companies also had to deal with the problem of measuring Spanish-speaking people. Arbitron found that using the personal-retrieval technique significantly increased the response rate in the Spanish community, especially when they used bilingual interviewers. The personal-retrieval technique did not work as well with Blacks. Thus, Arbitron used a telephone retrieval procedure that involved call-backs to selected households over a 7-day period to document listening habits. In essence, the interviewer filled out the diaries for those being surveyed. In 1982, Arbitron implemented Differential Survey Treatment (DST), a technique designed to increase the response rate among Blacks.

Birch/Scarborough Research uses special sampling procedures and bilingual interviewers to collect data from the Hispanic population. According to the company, its samples have yielded a high response rate among Blacks. Thus Birch has not utilized other special sampling controls. Ethnic listening reports containing average quarter-hour and cume estimates for Hispanics, Blacks, and others are available from the company in a format similar to that of its Capsule Market Report.

Both survey companies have employed additional procedures to survey other non-telephone households, especially in markets that have a large student or transient population.

The proliferation of survey services has drawn criticism from broadcasters who feel that they are being over-surveyed and over-researched. When Arbitron introduced its computerized monthly ratings service (Arbitrends), the chairman of its own radio advisory council opposed the venture on the grounds that it would cause more confusion and create more work for broadcasters. He further contended that the monthly service would encourage short-term buying by advertisers. Similar criticism was lodged against Birch/Scarborough's own computerized service, BirchPlus.

HOW AGENCIES BUY RADIO

The primacy of numbers is best illustrated through a discussion of how ad agencies place dollars on radio stations. It is the media buyer's job to effectively and efficiently invest the sponsor's money, in other words, to reach the most listeners with the budget allotted for radio use.

The most commonly employed method determines the cost per point (CPP) on a given station. A media buyer is given a budget and a gross rating point (GRP) goal. The objective is to buy to the GRP goal, without going over budget, against a predetermined target audience, i.e., adults 25–54, teens, men 18–34, and so on. The CPP is derived by taking the total budget and dividing by the GRP goal, or total number of rating points the buyer wishes to amass against the target audience. Now, using the CPP as a guideline, the buyer takes the cost per spot on a given station and divides it by the rating it has to see how close to the total CPP the station is. This is where the negotiation comes in. If the station is way off, the buyer may threaten not to place advertising until they come closer to what the agency buyer wants to spend.

The other method used to justify station buying is cost per thousand (CPM). Using this technique, the buyer determines the cost of reaching a thousand people at a given station. The CPM of one station is then compared with that of another to ascertain efficiency. In order to find out a station's CPM, the buyer must know the station's average quarter-hour audience (AQH Persons) estimate in the daypart targeted and the cost of a commercial during that time frame. The computation below will provide the station's CPM:

$$\frac{\$30 \text{ for } 60 \text{ seconds}}{25 \text{ (000) AQH}} = \$1.20 \text{ CPM}$$

By dividing the number of people reached into the cost of the commercial, the cost per thousand is deduced. Thus, the lower the CPM, the more efficient the buy. Of course, this assumes that the station selected delivers the target audience sought. Again, this is the responsibility of the individual buying media for an agency. It should be apparent by now that many things are taken into consideration before airtime is purchased.

And now you know some of the story, to paraphrase radio commentator Paul Harvey. No sales rep should remain in the dark about the research her station uses to market itself. Find out as much as you can, and use the knowledge to enhance your presentation.

RATINGS TERMS

Here are some common ratings/research terms extracted from glossaries prepared by RAB and Arbitron.

Area of Dominant Influence (ADI): An exclusive geographic area consisting of sampling units in which a station receives the bulk of its audience.

Average Quarter-Hour Audience (AQH Persons): An average of the number of people listening for at least 5 minutes in each quarter-hour over a specified period of time.

Share of Audience (Share): The percentage of those listening to radio in the AQH that are listening to a particular station.

Cumulative Audience (Cume): The number of different (unduplicated) people listening for at least 5 minutes during a specified period.

Gross Impressions: The total number of exposures to a schedule of announcements.

Reach: The number of different people exposed to a schedule of spots.

Frequency: The average number of times the audience reached by an advertising schedule is exposed to a commercial.

Universe: The estimated total number of persons in the sex/age group and geographic area being reported.

Cost Per Thousand (CPM): The basic term used to express radio's unit cost.

Gross Rating Point (GRP): Gross impressions expressed as a percentage of the population being measured.

Cost Per Point (CPP): An expression of radio's unit cost using a rating point, which is 1% of the population being measured.

Sampling Unit: A geographic area consisting of a single county, a group of counties, or part of a county.

12

The Spec Tape

Let the medium sell itself. An effective spec tape can soften even the toughest resolve. Radio sales reps have the greatest sales tool of all—radio!

GETTING ARTFUL FOR THE CLIENT

Marshall McLuhan observed that space is the world created by sound. Meaning that sound defines the universe and is infinite. Well, to serve our purposes let's say that McLuhan meant that when working with audio (creating radio commercials) there are no boundaries. The sky is the limit.

Renowned American poet Stephen Vincent Benet, who wrote for radio in the 1930s and early 1940s, called the medium the *theater of the mind*, and producer, writer, and all-around brilliant guy Stan Freberg demonstrated this for the benefit of later generations. In the 1960s, Freberg produced a series of unforgettable promotional announcements for radio. In one spot, he converted Lake Michigan into a million-ton tub of hot chocolate crowned by a 700-foot high mountain of whipped cream and a 2-ton maraschino cherry. Stimulated by the artful use of words and sounds, the listener (client) forms her own images and suddenly the world's largest cup of hot chocolate is very real.

Here are what a few of the medium's top producers say about the art of audio in my text *Radio Production: Art and Science*.

> KZOUs Lee Kent states, Some people paint on a canvas, some on television with new paint programs. Some people create sculptures out of clay or bronze, and some produce art with vinyl or plastic. The production person rearranges magnetic particles on recording tape as a means of conveying his message, and all art is a message of some sort. The radio producer creates something that did not exist before. Artists create a world, and his or her art is further embellished by the listener's thought processes.

Radio production is an involving and demanding art form, "Television destroys man's most precious possession—his imagination," believes WJCLs Al Jennings.

> Radio, with its word pictures, encourages people to think, to imagine. It massages the grey matter, as they say. If the message is good, if it is truly artful, it will move the listener. Radio can create warmth, intimacy, laughter, and sadness. It can arouse the curious side of our nature.

Good radio production can liberate and educate. It can launch the imagination into limitless flight. Good production—good art—motivates and
inspires.

To Paul Henna, operations director at Dubuque, Iowa's WDBQ-AM, radio's
artistic potential exceeds that of video.

Well-done radio production is an art form just as television production
is. We have the ability to create vivid word pictures that can last longer
than the high-tech, fleeting images of television. When I teach my radio
production class at a local college I always play great commercials of
the past by the masters, like Dick Orkin and Stan Freberg, to acquaint
my students with radio's legendary creative forces. They are amazed at
how long radio production has been an art form.

Artful production is the result of hard work, reminds WBAQs Paul Artman.

You must master the tools of the profession before you can produce
something exceptional and uncommon. Mastery of the tools is the first
and essential step toward making something that exceeds the commonplace. Only with unremitting desire to make something special can
something special be made.

The true art of production is bringing pleasure and joy to the listener, says
WKKDs Chris Tood.

I guess it's the entertainment aspect of radio commercials that qualifies
them as a kind of art form. Your spots are successful if they hold the listener's interest throughout the spot set. We all know how hard that can
be in this push-button age. I finally settled on a production career
because you're actually creating something with the potential to bring
pleasure to others while helping sponsors sell their product. Unlike
deejay work, where the pressure to perform is intense and you have to
be *on* every three minutes, and unlike live news where you only report
on what others are doing, the production person can breathe life into a
piece of copy and in doing so please the station, sponsor, and listener.

Russ Eckerea of Minnesota's KWWK adds this interesting insight.

I believe most full-time radio producers are frustrated fiction writers,
frustrated actors, and frustrated stand-up comedians living in the same
body. When you get all these things percolating at once something outstanding usually occurs, like great commercials, for example. I think the
public, or more accurately the critics (whoever they are) neglect to see
the art that exceptional audio production contains. Maybe someday.

So, you ask, what does all this have to do with being a station sales rep? Everything. You can't be effective selling something that you don't fully understand, so
knowing what gocs into making an artful commercial gives you powers. Powers?
That's right. First, just knowing what goes into making a client's message work

gives you a greater appreciation for what you're selling. Second, you can apply what you know to prepare a commercial (spec tape) for a sponsor that sells.

WHAT'S A SPEC?

A spec tape is a commercial produced for a client on speculation. It is intended to motivate the sponsor to act, to buy. There are no guarantees that all the valuable time spent preparing a spec spot will pay off, but the very fact that you and the station took the time to produce a tailor-made commercial for a sponsor is usually perceived in a very positive way. Therein lies the intrinsic value of spec spots. They are seen as a station's commitment to a prospect or client, because the station invests *up-front*; it goes the extra mile, so to speak, without any guarantees of compensation for its considerable effort. That alone impresses most retail business people. They know time is money, and that writing and mixing a commercial certainly isn't done without expense to the station. So this is a good strategy.

> "Hello, Mr. Merchant. As I mentioned to you on the phone, X109 has produced a commercial just for your business that we feel is going to convey to our listeners the importance of shopping in your store. Give a listen, and if you feel as strongly about it as we do, we can get it right on the air."

Another particularly valuable aspect of spec tapes is they demonstrate to the sponsor the power of the medium to deliver a message. No matter how jaded a client may be, to hear his business's story told through the magic of well-produced sound is a satisfying experience. Of course, *well-produced* is the key.

A spec spot should never (or rarely) be the plan itself but rather an element of the plan. In other words, design a package you know will do the job for the client, then use the spec spot to seal the deal. Few clients buy simply because they like a spec spot, even though it has happened. It is up to the AE to save the client from himself in this situation—meaning, have a solid package to back the spot. A great spot without a sound strategy (pun intended) for its application is a sail without *airwaves*. No specs for specs' sake.

WHEN TO USE A SPEC

There are numerous occasions when a spec tape can be valuable. Perhaps the most common application of spec spots is on the call-back, following the *consultancy* visit. During the initial encounter, the sales rep has gathered information on the client that is used to prepare both the plan and the spec tape. Here's a partial checklist of questions you can address as a prelude to preparing an effective spec spot for a client.

What Advertising Approaches Have Been Employed?
Find out what the client has done in the past. What worked, and what did not? Which approach or concept did the client particularly like (if any), and why? Don't repeat the sins of the past. Spending valuable time, energy, and resources on a spec that contains an idea already used by a client

is a supreme waste. Don't enter a project blindfolded, you'll fall over yourself.

What Type of Image Does the Client Seek to Convey?

Preparing a spec spot that fails to embrace a retailer's long established image can be both bad and good. In the first instance, if the prospect is married to an image of his business, presenting a spec that does not concur with that image can create considerable resistance. On the other hand, a strong spec may motivate a client to revamp his store's image, which may be the best thing possible. Tired images can do more to harm an enterprise than help it. It may seem cowardly to suggest this, but offering a fresh approach to an existing image is probably the better strategy. Don't try to reinvent a store without the proprietor's imprimatur, but don't be afraid to offer innovative, constructive suggestions either.

What Is the Personality of the Client?

Attempt an evaluation of the client's psyche. Get to know his personality. This will give you an idea of what direction to head in and how far you can go with an idea.

What Ideas Does the Retailer Have?

Query the retailer. Probe her creative reserves. See if the client is in possession of an idea and is excited about it. How can a prospect say no to her own brilliant concept? And sometimes they are brilliant, or at least viable. Working a client's idea is an almost certain way to generate his enthusiasm—and enthusiasm begets sales.

What Is the Look of the Store?

Play off the appearance of the store, if possible. "Drop by the world's biggest shoe store for the world's greatest values." If the store is unattractive or lacking in visible charm, work some other aspect, but if there is something unique about the appearance, exploit it. "Stop by the big red house to save some big greens." This falls into the make-the-most-of-what-you-have category.

What Products Are Featured?

It is a given that a spec tape highlights, if not spotlights, what the retailer is selling. To make no mention of the product is to talk about a car dealership without mentioning the kind of car it sells. Find out what the retailer is *pushing* (the store's featured item(s)) and give it play in your copy. Be relevant.

Where Is the Store Located and What Are Its Hours?

This is basic but vital information. Even the most innovative announcement must contain such essential data. It does no good to grab the listener with a great spot then fail to deliver on the particulars—where and when. A spec spot should be a super concept, but it must contain the vital statistics.

What Is the Retailer's Competition?

Determine the strengths and weaknesses of the retailer's competition and build
your spec accordingly. "Unlike the other guys, Saul's House of Ties is
open every night until 10:00 P.M. And unlike the other guys, Saul's
offers plenty of free parking. When it comes to ties, the other guys are
knots."

What Problems Exist?

Ascertain what the client perceives as the major problem or obstacle that blocks
the success he is after, and prepare a spec spot that addresses it. "So
we're a little hard to get to, but the money you save will more than
make up for the few extra minutes it takes to get to Saul's. You'll see
it's worth the effort…"

Sales reps also employ spec spots when attempting to increase a buy.

"The production staff at X109 came up with a really unique and novel
commercial concept for you. I think you're going to love it and want to
double up on your morning drive schedule for the next few days. Here,
give a listen…"

A great idea in a spec is pretty irresistible and can inspire a deeper investment
from the sponsor.

Spec spots are useful when attempting to re-sign a client. Approaching a client
with a fresh and exciting commercial certainly enhances chances of a positive
response.

Finally, when all else has failed, an ingeniously conceived and produced spec
can turn the tide. Pay careful notice to the word *ingeniously.* No hardliner is going to
collapse into giddy submissiveness after hearing a *so-what* spec, but if anything can
move a retailer, it is a powerfully crafted message, and if you can get Dustin
Hoffman to announce it, all the better.

SPEC PRESENTATION

Typically, the station production person dubs the spec spot onto a cassette. It is
then played for the client at his place of business. The sales rep decides at what point
in the presentation to play the spot. This depends on the variables inherent in the
face-to-face pitch, although the sales rep should have an idea as to when to present
the tape. Depending on the situation, the spec may lead off the pitch or conclude it.
The former approach is more common because the spec usually has the effect of
making a client more receptive to the details of the plan. In other words, the spec acts
as a sort of lubricant if it's good. If the spec isn't the answer to the retailer's dreams,
however, the presentation may come to a premature end. It all comes down to the
issue of timing. Each situation is different, so choose your timing wisely.

INDUSTRY NOTES BY JAY WILLIAMS

Good copy is essential to successful advertising. And if you are responsible for writing the copy, the burden is on you to make certain that the
copy will attract customers for your client. Here are a few points to
remember when writing copy.

1. Make your first sentence count. Does it provoke interest? Is it interesting? Does it
   command attention? If your first sentence doesn't have it, you've lost the best
   chance of securing the listener's attention.

2. Keep your copy simple. The most eloquent ideas and thoughts are done in few
   words—love, security, beauty, and other complex emotions and thoughts. If these
   can be done simply, how difficult can it be to sell a leather coat? The truth is,
   writing simply and cogently takes time and more effort than being wordy and
   windy. The results are worth the effort.

3. Always write for an individual. Don't use words like many of you that refer to a lot
   of people listening. Your message is intended for a specific listener. Radio is a personal medium. Don't address your copy to a crowd.

4. Always refer to your client as they or by a specific name (using third person). First
   person always refers to the station.

5. Pare down the details. Store hours, telephone numbers, what credit cards they take,
   etc., is information that belongs in newspaper, yellow pages, or filler copy. Sure,
   get the essentials in, but then get on with the message. None of that detail stuff will
   make me go to the store, and by putting it in the copy you're wasting valuable time
   on trivia that could be used better in romancing the product or service, describing
   benefits or uses, or other relevant ideas. A typical radio copywriter would turn "I
   love you" into "I love you all day and even more at night, and especially on weekends when we're together and we have less to do than we do during the week."

6. Use a positioning line that describes the store or product. This will help the listener
   remember the store and also why he should go there. Hallmark Cards: "When you
   care enough to send the very best." It not only says what the cards are (quality), but
   tells you when to use them.

7. Use a locator. People are not listening to radio ads with scratch pads and writing
   down addresses, phone numbers, or store hours. They need to be able to visualize
   where the store is. No one knows the address of anything. Many people don't know
   where the streets are in their very own town.

8. Mention the store name and the location at least three times in a piece of copy.

9. When you're done writing, read the copy aloud to someone. This is the ultimate
   litmus test. If it reads well and communicates well, you've done a good job. Have
   the person you read it to tell you what your copy said. You'll be surprised at what
   they remember and what they don't.

10. If you don't have control over your client and have to get the copy approved before it goes on the air, read the client the copy yourself. Have the copy approved before it's put into production. If it has to be changed after it has been produced, you've wasted too much of everyone's time. By reading the copy to the client yourself, you can make the changes on the spot.

Good copy has many rewards. It gets results. It gets results because it is focused—easy for the listener to remember the important points. It's produced better because announcers instinctively know better copy and work harder making it sound good. No amount of production work can save a bad piece of copy.

13

▼ Co-ops and Trade-Outs

Retailers have advertising subsidies available to them from many of the manufacturers and distributors of the products they carry. An astute sales rep can use co-op dollars to entice prospects to sign-on or increase their existing budgets.

CO-OP SALES

It is estimated that over $600 million in radio revenue comes from co-op advertising. Co-op advertising involves the cooperation of three parties: the retailer, the manufacturer (or distributor), and the medium (radio). In other words, a retailer and manufacturer get together to share advertising expenses. For example, Smith's Sporting Goods is informed by the Gold Running Shoes representative that the company will match, dollar for dollar, up to 5 thousand, the money the retailer invests in radio advertising. The only stipulation of the deal is that Gold be promoted in the commercials on which the money is spent. This means that no mention can be made of competitive products. Gold demands exclusivity for its contribution.

Manufacturers of practically every conceivable type of product, from lawn mowers to mobile homes, establish co-op advertising budgets. A radio salesperson can use co-op to great advantage. First, the station AE must determine the extent of co-op subsidy a client is entitled to receive. Most of the time the retailer knows the answer to this. Frequently, however, retailers do not take full advantage of the co-op funds that manufacturers make available. In some instances, retailers are not aware that a particular manufacturer will share radio advertising expenses. Many potential advertisers have been motivated to go on the air after discovering the existence of co-op dollars. Mid-size retailers account for the biggest chunk of the industry's co-op revenues. However, even the smallest retailer likely is eligible for some subsidy, and a salesperson can make this fact known for everyone's mutual advantage. Figure 19 explains how retailers can benefit by participating in a co-op.

The sales manager generally directs a station's co-op efforts. Large stations often employ a full-time co-op specialist or the services of a company that focuses on co-op advertising monies. The individual responsible for stimulating co-op revenue will survey retail trade journals for pertinent information about available dollars. Retail associations also are a good source of information, since they usually possess manufacturer co-op advertising lists. The importance of taking advantage of co-op opportunities cannot be overstated. Some stations, especially metro-market outlets, earn hundreds of thousands of dollars in additional ad revenue through their co-op efforts.

Growing Interest in Radio Co-op

Radio's ability to reach and motivate your best prospects has generated increasing interest in Radio as a primary retail advertising medium, especially as the effectiveness of newspaper advertising continues to decline.

Retailers and manufacturers are looking for advertising vehicles which are intrusive, uncluttered, and effective—and Radio heads the list!

The number of co-operative Radio advertising plans available to retailers has increased more than 45% in just four years, with a 50% increase in plans which offer full 100% manufacturer reimbursement for qualifying Radio advertising programs!

CO-OPERATIVE RADIO ADVERTISING PLANS

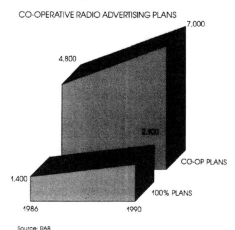

4,800

7,000

2,100

1,400

100% PLANS

CO-OP PLANS

1986   1990

Source: RAB

Co-operative Radio Advertising Increases Your Return

The best way to evaluate the return on an advertising investment is at the cash register, of course! But there are several ways to evaluate the potential impact of an ad campaign, and one is based on an analysis of "Reach" and "Frequency."

REACH: The percentage of the target group exposed to your ad at least once.

FREQUENCY: The average number of times the consumer is exposed to your ad.

Co-operative Radio advertising increases the Reach and Frequency of a retail ad plan using newspaper, without increasing cost! Compare these two media plans:

PLAN 1: Full-page ad in the "Anytown Gazette" (circulation 63,676). Cost: $4,000. Total retailer investment: $4,000.

Reach: 15%   Frequency: 1.0

PLAN 2: Half-page "Gazette" ad. Cost: $2,000—PLUS—"Full-page"-equivalent Radio co-op plan. Cost: $2,000 to retailer, and $2,000 to manufacturer (based on 50% allowance). Total retailer investment: $4,000.

Reach: 37.0%   Frequency: 3.4

That means **147% more people** are exposed to your ad and **240% more often**, at no extra cost to you! That's the power of Radio co-op to help overcome the declining effectiveness of daily newspaper!

▶ *Figure 19   RAB provides members with a myriad of data supporting radio advertising, including a useful booklet on co-op. Courtesy RAB.*

From the retailer's perspective, co-op advertising is not always a great bargain. This usually stems from copy constraints imposed by manufacturers that give the retailer a 10-second tag-out in a 30- or 60-second announcement. Obviously this does not please the retailer, who has split the cost of advertising 50–50. In recent years this type of domination by the co-op subsidizer has decreased and a more equitable approach, whereby both parties share evenly the exposure and the expense, is more commonplace.

Co-op also is appealing to radio stations since they do not have to modify their billing practices to accommodate the third party. Stations simply bill the retailer and provide an affidavit attesting to the time commercials aired. The retailer, in turn, bills the manufacturer for its share of the airtime. For its part, the manufacturer requires receipt of an affidavit before making payment. In certain cases, the station is asked to mail affidavits directly to the manufacturer. Some manufacturers stipulate that bills be sent to audit houses that inspect the materials before authorizing payment.

Co-op Glossary & Index

Accrual Co-op money earned by retailer as a percentage of purchases from manufacturer. Pg. 5.

Advertising Checking Bureau (ACB) Company used by manufacturers to audit retail co-op claims. Pg. 13.

Affidavit Statement, signed by station official, attesting that schedule was run as invoiced. Pg. 13.

Allowance Share of co-op advertising paid by manufacturer. Pg. 5.

ANA/RAB Radio Tear Sheet Radio co-op documentation system combining script with affidavit.

Cancellation date (also *expiration date*) Specific date when retailer's accruals are cut off. Pg. 5.

Co-op Partnership advertising where retailer, manufacturer and/or distributor share costs. Pg. 4.

Co-op Period Time period during which retailer purchases accrue co-op funds. Pg. 5.

Co-op Plan The manufacturer's formal offer to share advertising costs with retailer. Pg. 5.

Co-op Specialist (also called *Co-op Coordinator*) Radio station staffer who concentrates on co-op related business. Pg. 6.

Dealer A retailer who purchases manufacturer's products. Pg. 4.

Dealer Group An association of dealers who pool their co-op funds to finance a market-wide campaign. Pg. 10.

Dealer Support Program Local advertising program where manufacturer selects stations and schedules, and (usually) tags dealers. Manufacturer retains control rather than offering co-op.

Distributor (also called *wholesaler* or *jobber*) The middle man between manufacturer and retailer who sometimes administers co-op. Pg. 4.

Exact times Requirement made by some manufacturers requesting list of exact times commercials ran. Pg. 13.

FTC A free copy of "FTC Rules and Guides" (regulating co-op) is available from the Federal Trade Commission in Washington.

Horizontal Co-op A co-op program where several dealers' accruals are combined to fund a single schedule.

Manufacturer The company which makes the merchandise a co-op program promotes. Manufacturers are the source of co-op funds. Pg. 4.

Manufacturer's Rep The manufacturer's local representative. See page 4.

Notarization Certification by a notary public. Station affidavits are usually notarized. Pg. 13.

Pinpoint Marketing Company used by manufacturers to audit co-op.

Proof of Performance Evidence that the retailer ran co-op schedule as stated. Pg. 13.

Reimbursement Process where manufacturer repays retailer for its share of co-op costs. Pg. 5.

Vertical Co-op Co-op program which combines a retailer's accruals from various manufacturers to fund a schedule or campaign. Pg. 8.

Verification Manufacturer's system to confirm that a co-op campaign was run in accordance with the co-op plan. Pg. 13.

▶ *Figure 20   A glossary provided by RABs co-op. Courtesy of RAB.*

Figure 20 lists some commonly used co-op terms.

TRADE-OUTS

Stations commonly exchange airtime for goods, although top-rated outlets, who sell time for a premium price, are less likely to swap spots for anything but cold, hard cash. Rather than pay for needed items, such as office supplies and furniture, studio equipment, meals for clients and listeners, new cars, and so forth, a station may elect to strike a deal with merchants in which airtime is exchanged for merchandise. There are advertisers who only use radio on a trade basis. A station may start out in an exclusively trade relationship with a client in the hope of eventually converting him to cash. Split contracts also are written when a client agrees to provide both money and merchandise. For example, X109 needs two new office desks. The total cost of the desks if $800 dollars. If a client receives a $14 hundred ROS spot schedule in exchange for the desks, the station receives $600 hundred in cash.

Trade outs are not always this equitable. Stations often provide trade clients with airtime worth two or three times the value of the merchandise in order to get what they need. Thus the saying, "Need inspires deals."

Many sales managers also feel that it makes good business sense to write radio trade contracts to fill available and unsold airtime rather than let it pass unused. Once airtime is gone, it cannot be retrieved, and yesterday's unfilled availability is a lost opportunity.

Abuses of trade-outs have made for some pretty bizarre and amusing tales, like the one about the station manager who traded airtime for a new house, station wagon, recreational vehicle, clothing for his family, several vacations, and retirement care in Florida for both his and his wife's parents. Although the manager was found out and dismissed, the station was left holding the bag. The concept behind trade-outs is a good one, but control must be exerted, or a station can find itself in serious trouble.

INDUSTRY NOTES COURTESY OF RAB AND WOOD AM/FM

Co-op Made Easy

1. What is co-op?

    Sharing of advertising costs among retailer, distributor, and manufacturer that moves merchandise and makes money for all concerned.

2. Does a manufacturer have to approve all media in his co-op program?

    No. But most do approve radio, newspaper, television, and direct mail.

3. What kind of advertising allowances are usually available from manufacturers and what do they mean?

Plan	Mfg.	Retailer	Meaning
50–50	50	50	Accrued funds are matched by retailer.
2/3–1/3	2/3	1/3	Retailer pays 1/3.
75–25	75	25	Retailer pays 1/4.
100	100	0	Manufacturer pays all advertising costs up to accrued amount.

    Some plans provide for a three-way sharing: manufacturer, 50%; distributor, 25%; or some other arrangement.

4. If a manufacturer has a co-op program, may he specify different allowances for different media?

    Yes, but this is much less prevalent than it used to be now that radio has a well-accepted documentation: the ANA/RAB *tear-sheet*.

5. What is an accrual?

    The amount of money (or credit or merchandise) retailer earns for co-op that is usually based on his purchases of merchandise in the current or preceding year. Accrual percentages range from fractions of 1% all the way up to 25% of purchases depending on category of merchandise. If a plan is *unlimited*, co-op funds are not based on accruals but on a ceiling.

6. What are typical co-op periods?

A calendar year involves two periods: usually January 1–June 30 and July 1–December 31 and sometimes periods that begin with company's fiscal year.

Promotional (or deal) periods are typical of drug and grocery co-op plans. These are times designated by the manufacturer when he wants retailer to buy and/or advertise merchandise.

7. What is a distributor?

The middle man between manufacturer and retailer who supplies merchandise. Distributors may handle one manufacturer's products exclusively or (more usually) several manufacturer's products in the same category.

8. What is a manufacturer's rep?

The company's local representative with responsibility for selling merchandise, planning retailer advertising and sometimes determining co-op.

9. Two kinds of co-op organization explained.

Horizontal: several manufacturer's dealers band together to advertise the same product at the same time. The association is usually called a dealer group and is ordinarily organized by the manufacturer's rep working with a media rep.

Vertical: one retailer uses several manufacturers' co-op in a continuing advertising program.

10. What requirements do manufacturers usually make for co-op in advertising?

- Retailer (in most cases) must submit manufacturer's co-op form for permission to advertise.
- Only manufacturer products/brands mentioned in the co-op program may be co-opped. Some plans designate specific time periods the ads must run.
- Retailer must use manufacturer's radio scripts or tapes; or get prior approval for dealer copy in writing or over the phone. Some manufacturers pay higher co-op allowances or accruals when their scripts are used.
- Billing must follow the manufacturer's instructions to the letter. Many manufacturers now require the ANA/RAB radio *tear-sheet* (radio script with exact affidavit wording and notarized station official's signature plus a receipt of the station invoice) in order to pay co-op claim.
- Billing must be submitted to manufacturer directly or to her auditing firm (such as Advertising Checking Bureau or Pinpoint Marketing) by a specified date. The auditing firm either pays the bill (or okays it for manufacturer to pay) or sends it back to the retailer if documentation is incomplete.

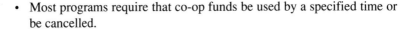

- Most programs require that co-op funds be used by a specified time or be cancelled.

11. What role does the FTC play in co-op?

The Federal Trace Commission's Department of Competition sets forth *FTC Rules and Guides* for co-op that manufacturers, retailers and media must follow to avoid unfair competition. A free copy of the *Guides* may be requested from the FTC, Washington, DC.

How Radio Stations Can Help You Use Your Co-op

Most of Radio Advertising Bureau's 3000 member stations have salespeople with special training in co-op. RAB publishes co-op directories that member stations use to stay up-to-date on manufacturer's co-op programs. Besides this, RAB conducts training seminars for new co-op salespeople in New York and in regional co-op meetings around the country. An RAB station works with a co-op retailer in much the same way an agency works with its clients except that the radio station's services are absolutely free. Here's a run-down on all the services a station can provide for a retailer in co-op.

- Research the products retailer carries that provide co-op.
- Write or call manufacturer's corporate headquarters and get a copy of the co-op program to be sure that all co-op rules are followed. If the retailer has the plan, no need for station to request it.
- Get retailer's accruals from the manufacturer as well as radio scripts or tapes.
- Plan a radio campaign based on retailer's available accruals and present proposal to retailer.
- Write copy if retailer prefers dealer copy to manufacturer's copy. Then get okay from manufacturer to run dealer copy.
- Inform retailer when spots will run so he may listen.
- Provide point-of-sale material in some cases; even devise contests or drawings to build traffic in the store.
- Furnish documentation (scripts, affidavits, invoices, ANA/RAB radio *tear-sheets*) whatever manufacturer requires.
- Meet with retailer after campaign to assess results and discuss on-going co-op plans.

If a retailer hasn't sufficient accruals to run a Radio campaign, the station co-op specialist will probably suggest putting together a dealer group where retailers pool their accruals and advertise together. If this is the case, it's quite likely that the radio co-op specialist will get in touch with the manufacturer's rep for help in organizing the manufacturer's dealers.

Ways Radio Co-op Specialist and Manufacturer's Rep Can Work Together

- The manufacturer's rep contacts his dealers and talks about the Radio proposal (which the co-op specialist would have outlined to him in writing).

Or the manufacturer and radio reps call on the dealers together to make the radio presentation and sign up those who wish to participate.

- Another possibility is a party or group meeting of dealers organized by station and manufacturer reps at the station or local motel. Station personality could be on hand to do the commercial being run by the group.
- In some dealer groups the manufacturer rep freezes the dealer's accruals and pays the station for the Radio time instead of having to collect individually from each dealer. Even if this isn't practical, the rep usually cooperates by furnishing accruals available from dealers so co-op specialist can plan the campaign around a realistic budget.

Once dealers and manufacturer's rep approve the dealer group program, the station performs all the services listed in the previous section *How Radio Stations Can Help You Use Your Co-op.*

This outline of what stations can do for manufacturer's retailers assumes that the station contacts dealers and reps. But it works the other way around, too. Often retailers contact radio stations they feel will best reach their customers and ask for their help in using co-op. Or manufacturer reps will contact radio station co-op people and ask them to help put a dealer group together.

The point is that radio stations are well-versed in handling co-op programs from beginning to end. They'll do a good job. For more information contact RAB's Co-op Department in New York.

14

What Makes a Good Salesperson?

The difference between the impossible and the possible lies in a person's determination—Tommy Lasorda

ON BECOMING AN AE

A notion held by some managers is that salespeople are born and not made. This position holds that a salesperson either has it or doesn't: *it* meaning the innate gift to sell, without which, all the schooling and training is of little help. Although this theory is not embraced by all sales managers, many agree with the view that anyone attempting a career in sales should first and foremost possess an unflagging desire to make money, because without it failure is almost assured.

During an employment interview between a station sales manager and a prospective sales rep the following is not considered a good response to the question "Why do you want to go into radio sales?":

"I want to help feed the hungry and shelter the homeless."

While human compassion is an important attribute, it generally does not top the list of sought-after qualities in a sales rep. The sales manager is likely to advise the job candidate to join the Peace Corps.

According to RAB figures, 70% of the radio salespeople hired by stations are gone within three years, a figure comparable to the turnover among new insurance salespeople. While this sounds less than encouraging, it also must be stated again that to succeed in broadcast sales invariably means substantial earnings and rapid advancement. True, the battle can be a tough one and the drop-out rate is high, but the fruits of success are sweet indeed.

WHAT THE SALES MANAGER LOOKS FOR

As part of the research for this book, I sent a questionnaire to over 100 station sales managers. It contained two questions: What skills must a radio salesperson possess to be successful on the direct-retail level? and What makes a *good* radio salesperson? What follows are responses to these questions from sales department heads and some successful AEs in small, medium, and large radio markets around the country.

What Skills Must a Radio Salesperson Possess to Be Successful on the Direct-Retail Level?

An account executive has to have a full understanding of what the retailer is trying to accomplish, what kind of budget is needed, and what dayparts the retailer should use to maximize her budget to get beneficial results. The account executive must not only be very knowledgeable about the client's product, but be able to map out the benefits of using her radio station and be able to pitch high rates and stick to them. So, on top of all the knowledge the AE must have, she must also have an eagle eye and always be searching for new business.

(Marc Kalman, general sales manager, WCCO-AM.)

A radio sales rep must be a self-starter, motivated by goals of achievement, including status items and money. I want a rep with integrity and good social skills. Someone who can deal with different types of clients and who is empathetic but persistent.

(Mary Ann Bosley, sales manager, WCBC-AM.)

A salesperson must be able to guide the customer to the fulfillment of his expectations. This requires everything stated in this book, and more.

(Jay Ronn, sales manager, WPBK-AM.)

The retail level in particular requires a salesperson to possess conversational skills. To be effective you have to deal with all kinds of people, from secretaries to CEOs. You've also got to be able to think on your feet, be a creative thinker, and know how to type, spell, and smile. Actually, the most important thing required to sell direct is common sense.

(Martha R. Burns, sales manager, WDSD/WDOV.)

The skills to sell radio on the direct-retail level are many and varied. First and foremost, one must have the ability to listen. By listening to the needs of the retailer, the salesperson can learn most anything necessary to help the retailer market his business properly.

(Jerry L. Grant, general sales manager, KKCS/KWES.)

Good oral and writing skills are vital. Being able to use co-op and vendor sources to maximum effect are more important than many realize.   (Glen Lucas, director of sales, WBZ-AM.)

Communication skills are ever so important, especially since we sell a communication product. This may sound very basic, but all the product knowledge and education on earth will not be of help if this knowledge is not conveyed successfully to the potential customer.

(Roger Hager, general manager, KKLR/KWOC.)

A sales rep on the direct beat must possess guile. By this we mean the ability to create a parching thirst for what you have to offer. Knowledge of the product—client's and your own—is a must, or you're never going to succeed. Flexibility is important also. By this we mean the instinct to keep things moving—street savvy, if you will.   (sales staff, WCUZ.)

You have to be a quick thinker and aggressive. Communication skills have to be high, and your ability to work with others must be strong. On top of it all put perseverance—the drive to keep going, keep calling.
(Shelly Meyer, KFMZ.)

In my opinion these are some of the skills a sales rep must possess to survive and succeed on the direct-retail street: enthusiasm, understanding of how businesses (the client's) operate, insatiable curiosity, vast awareness of area (locality), creative flair for problem solving, the ability to express concepts verbally and in writing, and a passion for radio.   (Edward Krovitz, general sales manager, KMGX/KGIL.)

Here are the skills or attributes that top my list: flexibility, solution and service orientation, capitalist bias, leisure and pleasure motivation, self-motivation, listening ability, team worker, appreciation for the product, and mastery of the language, to mention only a few.
(Jay Williams, president, Broadcasting Unlimited.)

I think we all have a list of what it takes to make it in this business. Here are some things I don't think you can function without: professionalism, tenacity, empathy, resilience, patience, creativity, integrity, affability, adaptability, articulation, and consistency.   (Linda S. Holter, KFMZ.)

What Makes a Good Salesperson?

A good salesperson will base his presentations on the relationship between facts and benefits. The formula that is most effective for good salespeople is (a) stress the benefits of advertising, (b) stress the benefits of radio advertising, (c) stress the benefits of advertising on your particular station. Furthermore, a good salesperson will not let a *no* be her demise. You must be willing to invest extra time to succeed. Sales requires long hours and tremendous effort that rarely fits neatly in a 9–5 day.   (Gary DeSantis, national sales manager, WOOD AM/FM.)

Courage! Courage is what makes a good salesperson.
(Jerry Frentress, sales manager, KRMD.)

A good salesperson is one who believes, without question, in the radio station she is selling. The radio sales rep doesn't have to have a profound appreciation for the station's format, but she must believe that what they have to sell will produce the best results for the client. The best radio people have a strong desire to please both their client and their station (and thereby themselves). Most good radio salespeople start out at a small station with little or no list at all and spend the first year bumbling through the territory. Along the way they usually encounter another salesperson they wish to emulate. Then the real development begins. Once the new sales rep learns what works well, she begins to fine tune and expand her skills. I guess a good salesperson really evolves.   (Martha Burns, WDOV.)

What makes a good *radio* salesperson is someone who has sold other things. Being out in front of the public, especially in a selling situation, regardless of the product, is excellent training for the prospective radio sales rep. I started in the transportation industry, first in customer service, then in sales. After that, I owned and operated a restaurant. Radio sales was a whole new ball game for me when I went to work for WCFR in Vermont in the mid-1970s. Having dealt with the public for two decades served me well. In two years, I rose to the station's top biller by concentrating mainly on direct-retail sales. In 1979, WKVT in Brattleboro hired me as sales manager.   (Charles Friedman, WKVT.)

A good salesperson is one who understands the advertising/marketing industry. A good salesperson is interested in helping advertisers develop a sensible marketing plan that instills front-of-the-mind awareness in their customers. Front-of-the-mind awareness in listeners eventually translates into increased customer traffic. A good sales rep acts in the best interest of both sponsor and station. This is a person who takes a creative approach to advertising.   (Jerry Grant, KWES.)

A salesperson who succeeds has all the product knowledge there is available, as well as an absolute belief in that product. Then that person has the initiative and ability to convey that message to the customer. A good salesperson sells himself to the customer before he sells the station.   (Roger Hager, KWOC.)

In this business, to be effective, you must have the ability to balance all areas of your life and keep a positive attitude. A healthy ego and solid self-esteem often are characteristic of a good sales rep.

(sales staff, WCUZ.)

You have to be able to read people and judge what methods work best with a client. An innate sense of timing—when to apply certain tactics—is necessary.   (Shelly Meyer, KFMZ.)

As a sales manager I value the following: experience in the areas of concept sales, radio sales, local clients contacts and agency contacts; knowledge in radio, advertising, business, agencies, and research; and creativity and presentational/communication talents.

(E. Krovoitz, KGIL.)

Everybody has an opinion of what constitutes a good salesperson. One thing should be clear, a good sales rep is a very special person. Unfortunately, contemporary society often lacks sufficient respect for this unique field of endeavor and the people who are its professionals. No matter. As comedian Billy Crystal used to say, "You know who you are."

VERTICAL AND HORIZONTAL OPPORTUNITIES

In recent years, sales managers have recruited more heavily within the radio station rather than looking outside for salespeople. For decades it was felt that programming people were not suited for sales. An inexplicable barrier seemed to separate the two areas. Since 1980, however, this attitude has changed to some degree, and sales managers now give serious consideration to on-air people who desire to make the transition to sales. The major advantage of hiring programming people to sell a station is that they have a first-hand understanding of the product.

Realizing that sales is the most direct path into station management, programming people often are eager to shift. In the 1990s, there is an even greater trend to recruit managers from the programming ranks. However, a sales background is preferred.

The salesperson is invariably among the best paid members of a station. How much a salesperson earns is usually left up to the individual to determine. Contrary to popular opinion, the salesperson's salary generally exceeds deejays, especially in smaller markets. In the larger market, certain air personalities' salaries are astronomical and even surpass the general manager's income, but major market sales salaries are commonly in the high 5 and even 6 figure range.

Entry level sales positions are fairly abundant, and stations are always on the lookout for good people. Perhaps no other position in the radio station affords an individual the opportunity that sales does, but most salespeople will not go beyond entry level sales. Yet for those who do hang in there, the payoff is worthwhile.

Incidentally, here are some interesting statistics on the radio sales field from a study by the University of Missouri for RAB. (This data is excerpted with permission from *The Pulse of Radio*.)

- 27% of radio sales managers are women vs. only 7% in TV sales.
- 48% of Radio salespeople are woman (TV 39%).
- Radio sales turnover in the last 12 months averaged 37%; in small markets 43%. Both figures are higher than any other industry measured by *Sales and Marketing Management*.
- 74% of respondents said their sales managers carried lists. They were evenly divided as to whether they felt positive, negative, or neutral about this.
- Sales contests were in use at 79% of the stations. Contests were liked or liked a lot by 59% of salespeople surveyed.
- Stations averaged two sales meetings a week, and 53% of the salespeople favor them. Those who dislike the meetings often said there was too much budgetary information and not enough brainstorming.

- Key motivators for salespeople: money, recognition, achievement, client satisfaction, and contests/incentives.
- Key motivators for sales managers: money, acceptance or belonging, professional goals, benefits, and meetings.
- Salespeople's most common likes: co-workers, management, money, work environment, freedom.
- Salespeople's most common dislikes: management, office politics, commission system, office communication, and paperwork.
- 81% of salespeople in markets 1–99 are paid straight commission or draw-against-commission (markets 100+ 61% are compensated that way). But the study says this is the least effective means of motivating the staff.

INDUSTRY NOTES BY DAVE GIFFORD

The following is an evaluation checklist of radio sales candidates. Managers circle the appropriate descriptions to arrive at an assessment of a would-be sales rep:

- Concerned with appearance or indifferent
- Loyal (to current employer) or disloyal (Who's next?)
- Charismatic or vanilla
- Open or suspicious and/or defensive
- Natural or affected
- Self-confident or unsure
- Good natured or hostile
- Good sense of humor or dull
- Positive or negative
- Enthusiastic or cheers down party
- Mature or immature
- Responsible or unreliable
- Intelligent or stuck for answers
- Clear thinking or confused
- Analytical or it's anybody's guess.
- Imaginative or plodding
- Problem solver or problem maker
- Well-mannered or crude
- Deliberate or impulsive
- Real-world patient or plays-the-ponies
- Opinionated or of no opinion
- Ethical or buyer beware
- Empathetic or judgmental
- Good-people skills or poor-people skills
- Assertive or shrinking violet
- Fluent or inarticulate
- Persuasive or easily persuaded
- Self-motivated or needs more tapes
- High-comfort or low-comfort zone

- Success-driven or security-driven
- In search of excellence or mediocrity
- Competitive or non-competitive
- Industrious or indolent
- Self-sufficient or dependent
- Persevering or easily discouraged
- Mentally tough or rollover
- Risk taker or habit-bound
- Adventurous or cautious
- Doer or dreamer
- Realistic or naive
- Well-organized or wheel spinner
- Decisive or vacillating
- Good judgment or blunders
- Overachiever or underachiever
- Knowledgeable or full-of-bull
- Willing to learn or intractable
- Gains from experience or never learns
- Team player or self-centered
- Leader or follower
- Manageable or unmanageable
- Asked good questions or lacks an inquiring mind
- Good listener or bad listener
- Frank or evasive
- Truthful or less than truthful

Here are some *must haves*:

- A success-driven orientation (ambition)
- Willingness to pay the price of success (competitive resolve)
- Commitment to excellence (fierce pride)
- High ethics (honesty)
- Responsibility to others, clients, company (maturity)
- Ability to get along with people (relationship and interpersonal skills)
- Assertiveness and persistence (risk taking and determination)
- Ability to communicate (questioning, listening, verbal and writing skills)
- Analytical ability (intelligence)
- Problem-solving/decision-making ability (good judgement, common sense)
- Compulsion to persuade (conviction)
- Creative ability (imagination)
- Planning and organizational skills (discipline)
- Willingness to learn (scholarship orientation and an inquiring mind)
- Evidence gained from experience (applied knowledge)
- Enthusiasm (a positive attitude)
- Most important (if applicable): a track record in new business development
- Bottom line: You've got to like, trust, and respect your salespeople

Here are some knockout considerations.

- 3+ jobs in the last 5 years
- Income requirements impossible to fulfill
- A string of low-paying positions
- Underqualified or overqualified
- Contradictory and/or untruthful answers or statements
- Missing information and/or time gaps on the resume
- History of failure
- Excuses
- Whatever your gut tells you (but check with legal counsel first)

INDUSTRY NOTES BY SKIP FINLEY

A retrospective on a selling life:

"Little did I know" doesn't quite sum it up but allows me to recall what an arrogant young SOB I was. I had been a sales trainee at WRKO-AM in Boston in December 1972 and was now officially an account executive. John Papas and Peter Crawford (my general and sales managers) left me unsupervised long enough one day earlier to go out and sell $2,000 worth of spots to DeMambro Electronics, a stereo store. They called it beginner's luck upon my return and cussed me out for misrepresenting myself as a salesperson. I acted appropriately chastened, but was extremely proud inside. WRKO had about a 60 share of teens, a 25 share overall and was the number two radio station only to Westinghouse's powerhouse, WBZ-AM. And I planned to bust my butt to become the number one biller at *Boston's Rocker.*

Management's directions for the Monday of my first week of sales were to canvas Boylston Street—one of the largest retail streets in Boston—and not return to the station until I had a sale or until 4:30 P.M. that Friday. "No problem," I recall thinking.

At about 4:35 P.M. that Friday, I (almost literally) crawled back into the station forcing back tears. No sales. By my third call, a retailer had repeated my canned pitch—leaving me nothing to say. It was a very discouraging week, filled with rejection and complete humiliation. But John, Peter, and the sales staff was there cheering when I walked in...now I knew selling radio wasn't easy, and they were proud I had come back to learn how.

Radio sales is asking 40 people a week to buy...and 39 say "no." This is a tough business, and you gotta be crazy (and tough) to do this for a living. I can't imaging doing anything else.

There's no such thing as a 60 share in radio in the 1990s *anywhere* in the Top-50 markets. Little did I know back then, but unless something major happens in the next few years, only some twenty years later, many people will never even have heard of AM radio.

I'm not quite as arrogant. I'm glad I was there then, because it's good to be here now.

Suggested Reading

Since this book only serves as a primer, further reading will help deepen the sales rep's understanding of this multifaceted subject. Contact the RAB in New York City and the NAB in Washington, D.C. for excellent information on material related to radio sales. Listed below are some popular texts on the topic.

Bergendorf, Fred. *Broadcast Advertising*. New York: Hastings House, 1983.

Culligan, Matthew J. *Getting Back to the Basics of Selling*. New York: Crown, 1981.

Delmar, Ken. *Winning Moves: The Body Language of Selling*. New York: Warner, 1984.

Hagerman, William. *Broadcast Advertising Copywriting*. Stoneham, MA: Focal Press, 1990.

Heighton, Elizabeth J. and Cunningham, Don R. *Advertising in the Broadcast and Cable Media*, 2nd ed. Belmont, CA: Wadsworth Publishing, 1984.

Hilliard, Robert. *Writing For Television and Radio*, 5th ed. Belmont, CA: Wadsworth Publishing, 1991.

Keith, Michael C. *The Radio Station*, 2nd ed. Stoneham, MA: Focal Press, 1989.

Lange, Mark R. *Professional Radio Selling*. Vincennes, IN: The Original Company, 1989.

Murphy, Jonne. *Handbook of Radio Advertising*. Radnor, PA: Chilton Books, 1980.

Schultz, Don E. *Essentials of Advertising Strategy*. Chicago: Crain Books, 1981.

Shane, Ed. *Power Selling Tactics*. Houston, TX: Shane Media Services, 1990.

Sissors, Jack Z. and Surmanek, Jim. *Advertising Media Planning*. 2nd ed. Chicago: Crain Books, 1982.

Warner, Charles and Buchman, Joseph. *Broadcast and Cable Selling*, Belmont, CA: Wadsworth Publishing Co, 1991.

White, Barton C. and Satterthwaite, N. Doyle. *The Selling of Broadcast Advertising*. Boston: Allyn and Bacon, 1989.

NOTES